STRESS-FREE

ENGINE MAINTENANCE

STRESS-FREE
ENGINE MAINTENANCE

Duncan Wells and Jonathan Parker

ADLARD COLES

LONDON • OXFORD • NEW YORK • NEW DELHI • SYDNEY

ADLARD COLES
Bloomsbury Publishing Plc
50 Bedford Square, London, WC1B 3DP, UK
29 Earlsfort Terrace, Dublin 2, Ireland

BLOOMSBURY, ADLARD COLES and the Adlard Coles logo are trademarks of Bloomsbury Publishing Plc

First published in Great Britain 2022

A catalogue record for this book is available from the British Library

ISBN: PB: 978-1-4729-8855-3; ePDF: 978-1-4729-8853-9; ePUB: 978-1-4729-8856-0

2 4 6 8 10 9 7 5 3 1

Designed and typeset in PT Serif by Susan McIntyre
Printed and bound in China by Toppan Leefung Printing

All photographs by or on behalf of Duncan Wells and Jonathan Parker unless otherwise specified.

FSC
www.fsc.org
MIX
Paper from
responsible sources
FSC® C104723

To find out more about our authors and books visit www.bloomsbury.com and sign up for our newsletters

Contents

Acknowledgements

Thank you to all who gave support, advice and enthusiasm to this project.

- All at Bloomsbury: Liz Multon, Nick Hunter, Kate Beer, Clara Jump and Jenny Clark. Susan McIntyre, the designer, and Tracy Saunders, the illustrator.
- Andrew Adams of Parker Adams for help with shots and video.
- And of course thank you to Sue Parker for her tireless and excellent transcribing. We would have a Zoom meeting, record it and Sue would transcribe and have the text back with us in a flash so we could write it up.
- Rick Gray, who took shots for us on *Dorothy Lee*.
- All those who allowed us to clamber over their boats taking things apart and photographing them, Andy Hobbs, Ed Crosse.
- Thanks to Kevin Falck for casting his professional eye over things.

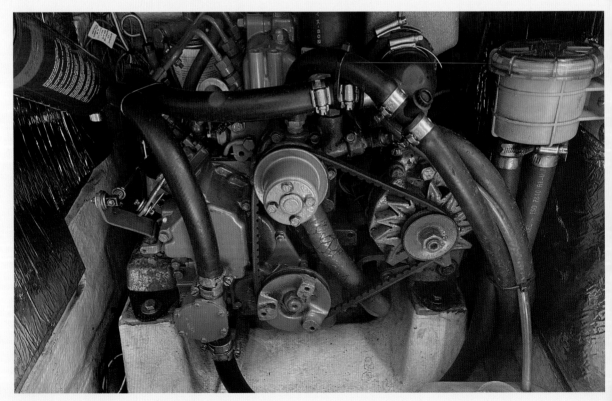

▲ *A tidy little engine and engine room.*

Preface

I met Jonathan at something of a low point in my boating life – when I ran out of fuel, or rather I didn't, as you will see. Jonathan was the Operations Manager of Sea Start at the time and he responded to my emergency call.

We were just heading out and about to raise the main when the engine coughed, spluttered and then stopped. What? It had no right to stop, it had just been serviced, there was plenty of fuel in the tank. I turned the key and the starter motor kicked in with plenty of force but the engine wouldn't fire up. It just turned over without catching. A blockage in the fuel line? Must be.

The fuel gauge on *Dorothy Lee*, having given up the ghost in 2008 or so, was still showing empty. As a result, I used to log the fuel and miles/hours in a book and I checked this. My crew, meanwhile, had unfurled the jib and we were sailing along nicely.

Even allowing for consumption at the rate of 5 litres per hour (lph) – unheard of, we normally do 3lph – we should have had around 80 litres in the tank.

More cranking with no success. Sea Start – the AA of the sea – were called. We were sailing up and down Calshot Reach, so it didn't take the Warsash-based Sea Start RIB long to reach us.

Any call-out for help is embarrassing, more so if your boat features in magazine articles, so I hoped we could get the thing fixed quickly, or at worst get towed in so we could sort things out on the dock rather more anonymously than out in the middle of the Solent.

Jonathan tied the RIB off to *Dorothy Lee* and we sailed up and down Calshot Reach for a bit while he went below to check the engine. A couple of crankings and a little putter as it began to start lifted our hearts, until it died a second later.

'I'm not sure what the problem is. It doesn't seem like there is any fuel in the tank', at which, out came my calculations and proof conclusive from me that there was fuel in the tank.

Jonathan was at a loss. So he towed us back to our marina berth. He called one of the other Sea Start RIBs that happened to be passing to see if they could help us get to the bottom of the problem.

Any chance of getting away with this quietly was blown as we now had two yellow Sea Start RIBs moored around our berth and, judging by the interested glances of neighbours, we were livening up everyone else's Saturday. Two Sea Start RIBS; it must be a serious problem.

Of course, I convinced everyone that there was something wrong with the engine. We couldn't have run out of fuel; I had records to show that there was fuel in the tank. No, there must be a fuel blockage. This had everyone flummoxed, Jonathan included. Air in the system meant no fuel in the tank.

'No', I said. 'There has to be fuel in the tank otherwise I have lost 80 litres and that's quite a bit to lose – you'd smell it, you'd think.' I was persuasive, there must be a blockage. I even got an engineer to fit a new electric fuel pump the next day. He brought with him a couple of litres of diesel and dropped this into the tank and with the new electric fuel pump the engine ran beautifully. The whole exercise was costing me a lot of money. And then with the engineer packed up and gone, a distant memory, the engine coughed, spluttered and died. What? Very odd. I checked the 80-litre reserve tank again and gave it a knock but I couldn't for the life of me tell if the knocking sound had a 'ting' to it to suggest empty, or a 'dong' to suggest full. Then I looked at the stopcock. It was closed. I must have dropped the tank and then closed it again, ready for the next fill-up. I'd better check. I opened the stopcock and the gurgling sound of 80 litres making its way to the main tank was unmistakable. Ah, so that's where the 80 litres were! Where the fuel should be. And I hadn't dropped the reserve into the main tank, as I had thought ... so the main tank was empty, just as Jonathan and everyone else had said. Oeuf sur le visage. Bum.

Moral of the story? Never listen to the owner or skipper on matters of fuel. ALWAYS dip the tank. To cap it all, I turned over the engineer's invoice for attending on the day of the 'incident' and then later to fit the new electric fuel pump and nearly fainted. This incident had cost me, all-in, very nearly £1,000, which included the penalty payment to Sea Start for having allowed my membership to lapse. There's a lesson to be learned in that right there.

Over the years I have relied on Jonathan's engineering skills and he has been kind enough never to mention the incident again. Jonathan's knowledge of boats and engines and what they do and what they don't do, is limitless.

And his engineering prowess is not limited to things mechanical. When I discovered the windscreen on my Hallberg Rassy had been smashed by something – how? It was as if someone had fired a gun at it, with a perfectly round hole in the middle and crazed glass around but no bullet evident– it was Jonathan who repaired it. I had knocked all the glass out and the windscreen had hinges so it could open and locking nuts to keep it closed but with no glass around, where you would drill the holes in the glass was anyone's guess. Jonathan worked out where the holes must have gone, ordered glass, fitted it to the not quite rectangular design of the frame and put the whole thing back together in a week. A tremendous feat of engineering.

Now, Jonathan and I have been wanting to write a book together for some time. Jonathan has a fund of stories about his Sea Start call-outs. Salutary lessons generally but very amusing at the same time. Of course, I am the subject of just such a salutary lesson.

And now we have found a vehicle. *Stress-Free Engine Maintenance* isn't about teaching you how to strip down a 4-cylinder diesel engine and then put it back together again. It is about showing why you need to look after the engine and how you need to look after the engine so that you avoid breakdowns. And if you do have a breakdown for one reason or another, showing you how to manage it and perhaps fix it yourself, regardless of how mechanically minded you may be.

There are videos throughout the book, which you can view by scanning the QR code on your smart device. You can also watch these videos online at westviewsailing. co.uk then click 'Stress Free Videos' and follow the link to 'Stress-Free Engine Maintenance'.

▲ *The smashed windscreen before I pulled all the glass out of it.*

▶ *The finished job. Perfection!*

Jonathan says

Warsash, midnight!

The phone rang.

'Sea Start. How can I help?'

'My engine keeps cutting out. There's no wind at all, it's completely died off and I am motoring. But the engine keeps cutting out.'

'OK, I'm coming. Where are you?'

'Biscay.'

'BISCAY! The Bay of Biscay?'

'Yes, I'm calling you on my satphone.'

'Right. Well obviously, I'm not coming. Can you tell me what it's doing?'

'Well it keeps petering out. It'll go for a couple of minutes and then cut out and then I give it a few minutes and it'll start up and then peter out again after another couple of minutes.'

'It sounds like a fuel problem.'

'Yes, I am sure it is but I just don't know what to do. I'm an accountant not an engineer. I haven't a clue when it comes to engines.'

At which point the satphone went dead. He called back five minutes later. This cutting out of the satphone went on for the next two and a half hours, during which time I got the chap to change both fuel filters, clean the fuel line out to the fuel tank, which is where the blockage was, and get the engine running again to get himself to shore in northern Spain.

I asked him a few questions about the engine, did it have a such and such here or a pipe there? I was pretty sure he was looking at a Volvo MD21B. I pictured the engine in my mind and then took him through everything step by step.

I'd ask him to describe the fuel filter and then I'd know what I was dealing with and could tell him exactly what to do, even to the point of taking a pipe off and blowing back into the fuel tank to try and clear the blockage on the assumption that this was the problem and would buy him some time to get to the shore.

'The fuel filter is a round filter, by the front of the engine up high on the left. Follow the pipe down from there and you come to the lift pump on the engine, now follow that to another pipe that comes down from the pre-filter on the bulkhead. That's the one that will block up if there is a blockage and is it a rubber pipe?'

'No, it's a copper pipe.'

'With small metal clips?'

'Yes, that's right.'

'They're jubilee clips. You need to take this apart. Have you got something to drain the fuel into?'

'Yes, I've got something.'

'Well put that underneath, now there's a drain on the bottom. Can you feel it?'

'Er ... yes, yes I can feel it.'

'Well drain that out.'

...and then the phone would cut out. Then five minutes later he'd call back. This continued for some time until he reached the filter in the fuel line.

'Now, is there any dirt on the filter?'

'Well, it's not that bad.'

'Then there must be a blockage in the fuel line, the line from the fuel tank to that filter, so undo the jubilee clip attaching the line to the filter. Now, blow down it and if you can feel a restriction just see if you can clear it.'

So he went off to do that and came back.

'Yes, it was quite hard and then suddenly it came free and I could hear the air in the fuel tank.'

'Great, you've unblocked it.'

And then he put it all back together again.

'Make sure you put the seals in right – they are a pain in the arse. Right, now you've got to bleed the engine. You need to undo the bleed screw, not the bolt that is in the centre of the engine; undo that and the whole thing will fall to pieces...'

And when we had finished and the engine was running smoothly once more, he was on top of the world. As pleased as punch with what he had been able to achieve. Starting off knowing nothing, he had been able to fix the problem. It would have taken the rescue services many hours to find him. It was fortunate that he had a satphone and thought of calling Sea Start.

I discovered later that he had had to repeat this process a further three times before he made harbour.

Introduction and philosophy

The idea of this book is to give you an introduction to engines on boats and their associated systems so that you can keep an eye on things and stay one step ahead of any problem.

It is not designed to train you to become a mechanic.

That said, we will take you through all of the essential jobs required to maintain your engine and indeed to service it. We will also outline what you need to check if a problem does arise, in order to fix it.

The key with all things mechanical, well anything really, is to stay on top of what they require to run properly, to look out for wear and tear and to replace a component before it wears out and fails. To think ahead.

A classic case in the domestic setting is when you leave batteries in a torch and then don't use it for years. When you do try to switch it on, it won't work and when you open it up you will find a nasty mess as the acid will have leaked out. The torch is now ruined. Had you removed the batteries when the torch was not being used then the torch would be ready to go as soon as you gave it some batteries with charge in them. So have a look round the boat, identify things that require batteries that you don't use often and remove the batteries – tape the batteries to the item so you have them to hand. Your safety gear, for example, lights on lifebuoys and danbuoys – remove the batteries.

Of course, you should never forget, when trying to work out what goes where, that the manuals that came with your engine will be an excellent resource and guide to tell you what to do.

We will be covering both petrol and diesel engines and we will also include other elements beyond engines that you should design a maintenance schedule for – parts that wear out, corrode or clog that you need to

keep an eye on. We can all be guilty of managing to keep up with the regular, advisory engine maintenance while ignoring other things that need our attention as well. We need to keep on top of every system, anything mechanical on the boat. Let's not wait for things to fail before we address them because that is no fun for anyone; let's maintain these systems and prevent problems from occurring in the first place. Your expensive electric windlass needs servicing, pumps for domestic fresh water, pumps for draining showers and pumps (automatic and manual) for bilges also need to be checked. Even the gas system: Is the regulator in date

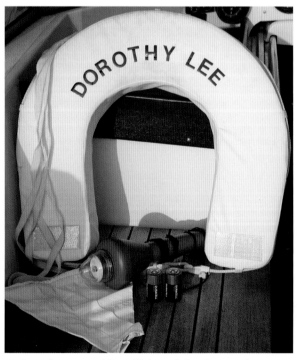

▲ *Batteries removed from lifebuoy light when not in use.*

and OK? Is the pipework in date and OK? And of course, alarms for gas, smoke and carbon monoxide. Then of course there is the fridge and freezer, not forgetting the generator.

Fixing things at sea means you will be working in a confined space, possibly with a strong smell of diesel and probably with your body straining at every sinew and bent to an impossible angle as you try to undo that nut at the back of the engine. Not the ideal position to be in if you are apt to feel seasick. The only time I have had a 'moment' was when I was upside down in a lazarette trying to fix something. I had to get my head out quickly and take a breath of fresh air before getting back to it.

As long as we stay on top of the servicing, treat our mechanical equipment with care, understand how to use it to get the best out of it and to reduce wear and tear, then we will be in good shape.

Finally, I – Duncan Wells – am the student here, the one who makes all the mistakes (and I do) and Jonathan Parker is the expert. And so everything on these pages has had to be filtered through the fog of my non-mechanical brain. If I was able to understand how something was described then that description was fit for the book.

You will find that there is tremendous emphasis on checking things and adhering to service schedules and the service life of parts and indeed repetition of the need for this. You see, *Stress-Free Engine Maintenance* is really about preparation – just like every aspect of sailing – identifying potential problems and heading them off before they occur.

The book is structured in such a way that when you get to the chapter 'How to troubleshoot a breakdown' and the flow diagrams, you will have been shown in the preceding chapters how to identify and check everything that is mentioned and how to fix it.

Jonathan always has a story to illustrate every point and we include these at the end of each chapter. We will also have some of Jonathan's life experiences 'en passant' throughout. These are not meant to be judgemental, in fact in most cases it is a question of 'There but for the grace of God go I', but they do drive home the point.

Jonathan says

The phone went in the Sea Start office and it was a sportsboat anchored in Osborne Bay, Isle of Wight.

'I can't start the engine and I need to get going. I've tried everything.'

He wasn't a member. We always took the view that if we weren't busy, we'd go out to anyone, but first the office had to take some details and take some money off him.

'Yes fine, fine, but I need to get going.'

With a membership fee and a call-out charge paid – which came to quite a lot – I started to ask him questions to see if we could get the engine started.

He was quite insistent that I should come and see him and he didn't really want to listen to what I was trying to tell him on the phone, he'd tried this, he'd tried that, he said.

So I said OK, I'd be there in about 10 minutes.

When I get there, he has all his family on this day boat and friends, about ten of them, and they were all looking expectantly at me. I glanced at the controls and then just moved the gear lever from forward into neutral and then fired up the engine. Well, the look his wife gave him told the whole story. And she said, 'Do you know how much that just cost me?' Clearly she had paid, as well!

I had asked him if it was in gear when I first spoke to him on the phone but for some reason he was panicking and just wanted me to come out and sort it. Had he listened, he could have saved himself, sorry his wife, a lot of money.

People often panic. They just don't think. One of the favourites is a call to say:

'My steering's jammed. It won't work.'

'Is the boat going round in circles?'

'No'

'Is it maintaining the heading?'

'What?'

'Is the boat steering straight ahead?'

'Yes'

'Do you have an autopilot?'

'Um, yes? Oh right. OK, everything's fine now!'

The caller has just realised that the autopilot is on and he is trying to fight it by steering the helm. With the autopilot off, he will regain control of the helm.

If the steering had really jammed, it would more than likely be steering the boat round in circles. Quite often, autopilots can be switched from standby to auto by people without them noticing. Autopilot controls on sailing boats are often set into the cockpit coaming where crew sit and, shuffling about, they can hit the auto-on button by accident.

Worth remembering – most motorboat engines won't start when they are in gear – it's a safety feature... or if the kill cord isn't attached. Most yacht engines will start when in gear.

Never drive a boat with a kill cord attachment if the kill cord is not attached to your wrist or thigh. Carrying a spare kill cord will enable a passenger to start the engine and pick up the original driver who fell out of the boat and is now 30 or more metres behind, with the kill cord still attached to them!

▲ *As it says...*

2 Principles of the engine

How does an engine work?

An engine works by converting heat into mechanical work.

A **steam engine** has a fire, which heats up water in a boiler to create steam. This steam under pressure pushes a piston along a cylinder. The piston is attached at one end, via a crank, to the wheels, which makes them go round. At the other end it is attached, again via a crank, so when it reaches the end of the cylinder it moves back down the cylinder – assisted by momentum – until pressurised steam pushes the piston back along the cylinder. A steam engine is an external combustion engine.

A **diesel** or **petrol engine** is an example of an internal combustion engine. Here the heat is created by exploding fuel and air in the correct ratio within the cylinders and that causes the pistons to go up and down.

The difference between a diesel and a petrol engine is simply the way in which the combustion takes place. In a diesel the combustion is a result of very high air pressure created by the piston in the cylinder, which raises the temperature of the air to the point at which diesel will combust. It is referred to as a 'compression ignition' cycle. In a petrol engine the combustion is started again with air being heated by being compressed in the cylinder but ignited by a spark from a spark plug. Because the petrol is ignited by a spark, a petrol engine does not need to compress the air in the cylinder to the same degree as a diesel. And so a diesel engine, which handles higher compression levels than a petrol engine, has to be made out of stronger, heavier materials and therefore weighs more than a petrol engine.

You can also get engines in cars that are powered by liquid petroleum gas (LPG) and these work in the same way as a petrol engine, with a spark to ignite the gas and air mixture, although they are rare in the marine world.

▲ Note diesel engine injectors.

▲ Note HT lead and spark plugs.

Types of engine

There are two types of engine whether we are talking diesel or petrol and these are four-stroke and two-stroke.

The manufacture of old-style two-stroke engines was banned in the EU from 2007 because they are not as environmentally friendly as four-stroke engines. Stroke, as you will see shortly, refers to the number of times the piston moves up or down inside the cylinder per power cycle and if the piston only moves twice for one cycle of the engine then it is unable to burn fuel efficiently and thus expels more particulates into the atmosphere than an engine that has four strokes per cycle. Of course, there are plenty of old two-stroke engines around, it is just that no one manufactures them any more. There are some larger two-stroke engines manufactured with special fuel- and oil-delivery systems, which make their emissions cleaner, but these tend to be very expensive engines.

The fundamentals of a four-stroke engine

All engines have a block that contains the cylinders and the pistons, which are attached to a crankshaft by connecting rods or 'con rods'. The actions of the pistons and the con rods turn the crankshaft, which turns a flywheel, and the momentum of the flywheel helps to keep the pistons moving.

Bolted to the top of the block is the cylinder head, in which are the intake and exhaust valves for air and fuel for each cylinder. These valves are controlled by the camshaft, which opens and shuts them in synch

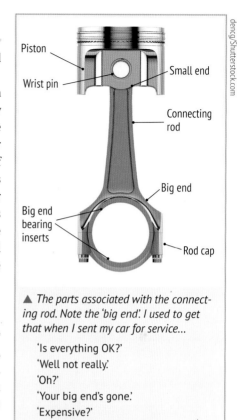

dencg/Shutterstock.com

▲ The parts associated with the connecting rod. Note the 'big end'. I used to get that when I sent my car for service...

'Is everything OK?'
'Well not really.'
'Oh?'
'Your big end's gone.'
'Expensive?'
SFX: Sharp intake of breath
'I should say so.'

THE WORKING PARTS OF AN ENGINE

1. Turning the key to start activates the starter motor, which turns the flywheel.
2. The flywheel turns the crankshaft and begins the compression ignition cycle as the crankshaft pushes the pistons and the camshaft in turn opens and closes the air inlet and exhaust valves.
3. At the same time, the drive belt driven by the crankshaft is used to turn any other ancillary components such as the alternator, which charges the battery, raw-water and fresh-water pumps, power-steering pumps and superchargers.
4. The crankshaft also powers the pressurised oil system via gearing to the oil pump, which lubricates the engine.

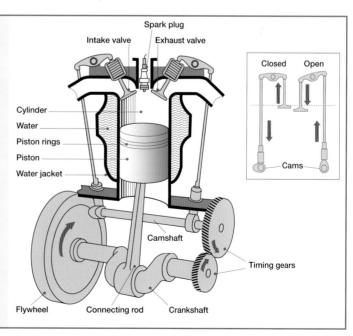

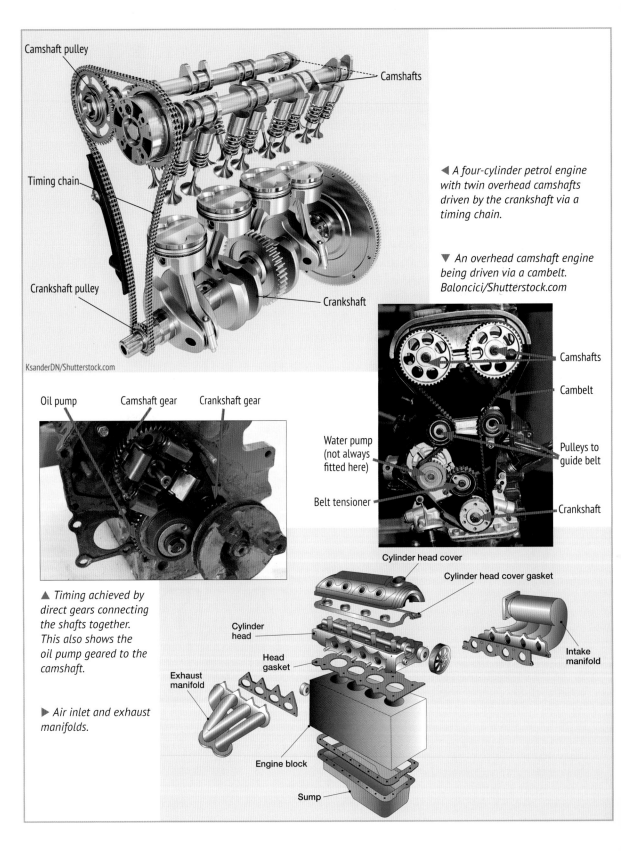

Camshaft pulley

Camshafts

Timing chain

◄ A four-cylinder petrol engine with twin overhead camshafts driven by the crankshaft via a timing chain.

▼ An overhead camshaft engine being driven via a cambelt. Baloncici/Shutterstock.com

Crankshaft pulley

Crankshaft

KsanderDN/Shutterstock.com

Camshafts

Cambelt

Oil pump   Camshaft gear   Crankshaft gear

Water pump (not always fitted here)

Pulleys to guide belt

Belt tensioner

Crankshaft

Cylinder head cover

Cylinder head cover gasket

▲ Timing achieved by direct gears connecting the shafts together. This also shows the oil pump geared to the camshaft.

► Air inlet and exhaust manifolds.

Cylinder head

Head gasket

Exhaust manifold

Intake manifold

Engine block

Sump

with the movement of the piston. The camshaft can be above the cylinders, where it will be in direct contact with the valves and there is no need for a rocker arm, or beside the cylinders, where it will operate the rocker arms via pushrods.

The camshaft is connected to the crankshaft either by a system of gearing or with a timing chain or cambelt.

At the bottom of the engine block is the sump where the engine oil is stored, ready to be sucked up and pumped around the engine.

Attached to the cylinder head is the inlet manifold to allow air into the cylinders and the exhaust manifold to allow combustion (exploded gases) out.

An engine where the crankshaft is directly geared to the camshaft will have the camshaft mounted in the cylinder block. As the camshaft turns, the camshaft followers push up and down on pushrods, which are connected to rockers mounted on the rocker shaft. The rockers then operate spring-loaded valves, which open and close in sequence. This type of engine is known as a pushrod engine. Pushrod engines can also have a short chain linking the crankshaft to the camshaft.

A pushrod engine gives you power – torque – at low speed, because it allows relatively large amounts of air by comparison with fuel into the cylinders at low revs. As the revs increase because you are introducing more fuel, so the ratio of air to fuel is reduced – you can only get a limited amount of air into the cylinder naturally. Engines where the air is introduced to the cylinder naturally are referred to as 'naturally aspirated' engines.

A way of getting an engine to 'breathe' more efficiently is by having two air intake valves and two exhaust outlet valves per cylinder. If you take a circular cylinder and cut two holes in the top – one for the intake valve and one for the exhaust valve – you quickly arrive at the largest holes you can have for the diameter of the cylinder.

If, however, you make four holes in the top of the cylinder – two intake valves and two exhaust valves – although they will each be smaller holes, their combined surface area will be greater than the two holes you had before. So, you can get at least 50 per cent more air into the engine and can achieve higher engine speeds. This setup requires a double camshaft which is sited on top of the cylinder block and is referred to as a double overhead camshaft (DOHC).

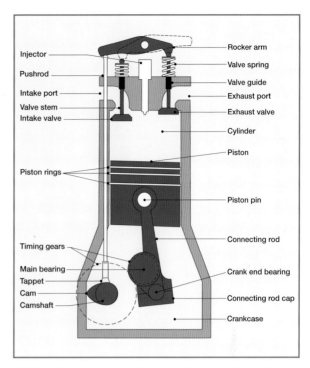

▲ *Directly geared camshaft mounted in the cylinder block showing camshaft followers and pushrods.*

More or less all larger outboard engines, over 90 horsepower (hp), will have double overhead camshafts. The benefit of a double overhead camshaft, apart from increasing the inlet air volume, is that it reduces the number of working parts in the engine. The two camshafts being in direct contact with their respective inlet and exhaust valves, there is no need for pushrods. This increases performance, particularly at higher engine speeds.

To increase the power, you need to add more air to the fuel and so you need to force air into the cylinder. Here there are two options: you can use a supercharger, which is driven by the engine via a belt, or you can use a turbo, which is driven by the exhaust gases. The difference being that a supercharger being run by the engine takes a load from the engine, whereas a turbo run by the exhaust gases takes no load from the engine. But a turbo needs a certain level of exhaust gas emission to become effective and so adds this extra air and power at higher speeds. A supercharger can be timed to cut in at lower speeds and thus increase the 'low-end torque' – power at low revs. But the trade-off for this is that at higher revs, although it will provide as much extra power as a turbo, it is using engine

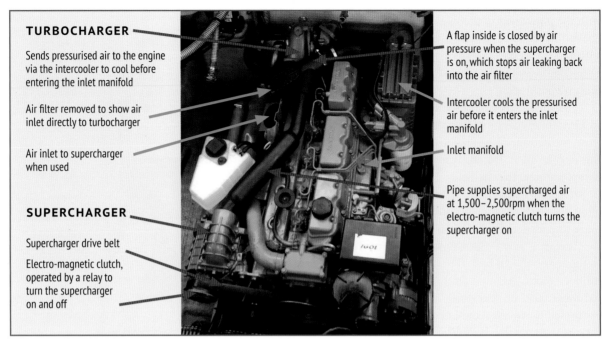

TURBOCHARGER

Sends pressurised air to the engine via the intercooler to cool before entering the inlet manifold

Air filter removed to show air inlet directly to turbocharger

Air inlet to supercharger when used

SUPERCHARGER

Supercharger drive belt

Electro-magnetic clutch, operated by a relay to turn the supercharger on and off

A flap inside is closed by air pressure when the supercharger is on, which stops air leaking back into the air filter

Intercooler cools the pressurised air before it enters the inlet manifold

Inlet manifold

Pipe supplies supercharged air at 1,500–2,500rpm when the electro-magnetic clutch turns the supercharger on

▲ *A Volvo Penta KAD series engine showing both supercharger and turbo.*

power to achieve this and therefore requires the engine to use more fuel and so is less efficient than a turbo.

The answer is, of course, to have both a supercharger and a turbo and there are some engines fitted with both of these.

Engines on boats have one forward gear and one reverse gear and different types of boat with various hull designs have different power requirements. Planing motorboats need sufficient power at low revs in forward gear to get the hull moving through the water and on to the plane and then a reverse gear, which will allow them to stop quickly. Whereas a yacht does not need to accelerate quickly and will never go faster than its hull displacement speed when under power and so you don't need a great deal of 'top end' power.

Picking the right engine option is very important to get the best out of the hull design. It is not only power we need to think about, it is also weight, weight distribution and propeller choice.

A planing boat can be the hardest hull design for which to find the optimum balance, because you want enough power to push the mass of the boat through the bow wave on to the plane but you also need the boat to be as light as possible to enable it to lift the hull out of the water and on to the plane. So most planing boats will either have a lighter normally aspirated petrol engine or if they opt for a diesel engine, which is much heavier than a petrol engine, then they will need to have it turbocharged and/or supercharged.

Propeller choice for a planing boat is also critical as it needs to provide a mix of low-speed torque to accelerate the boat on to the plane and bring it to a stop, as well as to enable the engine to rev to the correct full throttle speed when the boat is on the plane. When a boat is being commissioned, it is common to try two or three different propeller sizes to get the best from an engine.

The fundamentals of a two-stroke engine

Two-stroke petrol engines, where lubricating oil is added to the petrol, have been banned in Europe mainly because they are not as environmentally friendly as four-stroke petrol engines, where the lubricating oil is not added to the petrol but stored in a sump. Four-stroke engines have specific strokes devoted to separating the air coming in from the exhaust gases being expelled. A two-stroke engine does not. As a result, the fuel is not used efficiently and the exhaust gases are not as clean as those of a four-stroke.

HOW A PETROL TWO-STROKE ENGINE WORKS

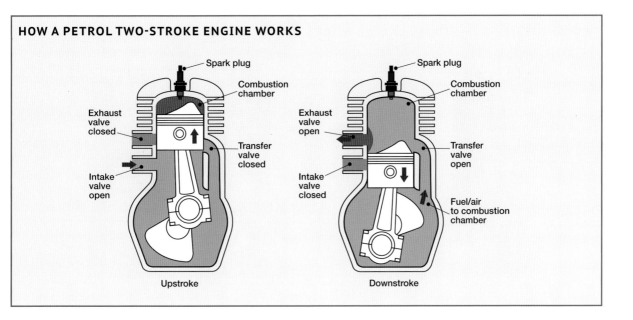

Spark plug

Combustion chamber

Exhaust valve closed

Transfer valve closed

Intake valve open

Upstroke

Spark plug

Combustion chamber

Exhaust valve open

Transfer valve open

Intake valve closed

Fuel/air to combustion chamber

Downstroke

You can still buy larger two-stroke petrol outboards such as Evinrude and some Mercury engines, but they now have a complicated fuel and oil delivery system where the oil is injected into the fuel, which makes for a more precise mixture and results in cleaner emissions, making them more environmentally friendly. This extra complication of course adds to the cost. As four-stroke engines are simpler and cheaper to produce, four-stroke petrol outboards in the main are more popular.

Two-stroke diesels work differently from two-stroke petrol engines in that they do not pre-mix the oil and fuel. Although rare in the leisure market, you can get two-stroke diesel engines – Sunseeker use the Detroit Diesel engine in some of their 'Manhattan' models. Just like a four-stroke diesel engine, the fuel in a two-stroke diesel engine is injected into the cylinder.

The benefit of a two-stroke diesel engine over a four-stroke is a weight saving. You see, a two-stroke engine produces its power at every second stroke of the piston travelling from one end of the combustion chamber to the other, whereas a four-stroke engine produces its power every fourth stroke of the piston. Because of this, a two-stroke engine can produce twice the power of a four-stroke engine for the equivalent size of engine, or it can be made half the weight to produce the same power. In practice, this is why a 4hp two-stroke outboard is lighter than a 4hp four-stroke and why they are sought after in the second-hand market.

As with the two-stroke petrol, it is difficult for a two-stroke diesel to clear the burnt fuel entirely after each combustion so these engines tend to smoke heavily, especially under acceleration. So in the leisure market the cleaner-running four-stroke engines are preferred.

How does a four-stroke diesel engine work?

'Suck, Squeeze, Bang, Blow', that's it.

A piston attached to a crankshaft runs up and down the cylinder, twice – that is four strokes in one power cycle. It starts at the top, valves closed, then as the piston travels down the cylinder the intake valve opens and air is sucked in (intake stroke 1st), then the intake valve closes and the piston goes back up the cylinder and squeezes this air, compressing it to between 15 and 22 times its original volume until it reaches more than 550°C which is hot enough to cause the diesel, injected when the air is fully compressed, to explode (compression stroke 2nd). The force of this pushes the piston down the cylinder (combustion stroke 3rd); the piston then rises up the cylinder and as it does so the exhaust valve opens and the exhaust gases are pushed out (exhaust stroke 4th). This is called the compression-ignition cycle.

Because diesel engines compress the air inside the cylinder to such a great degree, the metals used for the cylinders need to be very strong. This traditionally

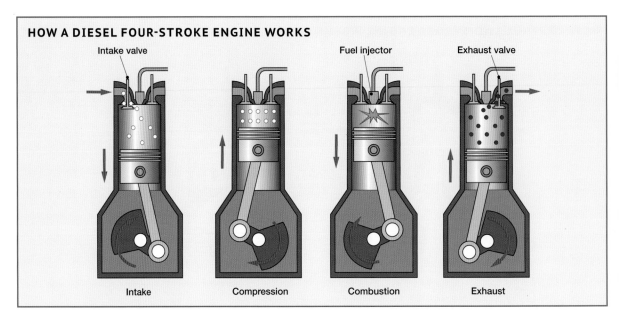

HOW A DIESEL FOUR-STROKE ENGINE WORKS

Intake valve   Fuel injector   Exhaust valve

Intake   Compression   Combustion   Exhaust

Four-stroke diesel engine

Stroke	Known as	Piston	Intake valve	Exhaust valve
1. Intake	Suck	Down cylinder, sucks in air	Open	Closed
2. Compression	Squeeze	Up cylinder, compresses the air, fuel injected	Closed	Closed
3. Combustion	Bang	Down cylinder as fuel and air combust, expanding gases in the cylinder	Closed	Closed
4. Exhaust	Blow	Up cylinder, blowing out the exhaust gases	Closed	Open

meant that the engines were heavy. That is why you will not until recently have seen diesel outboards. Today though, newer alloys, precise control of fuel injection and a more compact engine design have reduced the weight of diesel engines. As a result, diesel outboards are now becoming more popular.

◆ Starting a diesel engine

The cylinders, depending on their design, sometimes need to be pre-heated prior to cold starts and for this diesel engines use glow plugs. This may be a single glow plug, which will heat the air before it is sucked into the engine via the 'inlet manifold', or there may be a glow plug on each of the cylinders. Their purpose is to pre-heat the air within the cylinder so that when compressed it will reach over 550°C so the fuel will ignite on the first compression stroke of each cylinder. The glow plugs are

connected to the electrical system and the ignition key or a button is pressed for a number of seconds to heat them up before the ignition key is turned to engage the starter motor which turns over the engine. Diesel is then introduced via a fuel injector in the top of the cylinder, to coincide directly with the point that the air is fully compressed on the 'compression stroke'.

◆ Increasing the engine speed

This is done by introducing more fuel. The more fuel, the bigger the bang, the greater the engine speed and power. The air that is required to allow combustion is drawn in via the air filter and inlet manifold and has an uninterrupted flow, ready for the intake valve to open and the piston to suck the air in on the intake stroke. Any increase in engine speed and power is done by increasing the amount of diesel injected and the extra air will suck

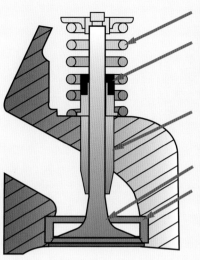

These are valve stem oil seals, which you need to check, because if they leak you will get blue smoke.

Valve spring - returns the valve to its closed position.

Valve stem oil seal - stops the majority of the lubricating oil above from leaking into the combustion chamber when the valve is open, but allows a small amount to help lubricate the valve guide.

Valve guide - a replaceable part that is changed when the valve guide wears out by friction, eventually affecting the valve's position on the valve seat.

Valve - either intake or exhaust valve.

Valve seat - the valve is ground into here with grinding paste to create an airtight fit that seals the combustion chamber when closed. This is essential otherwise full combustion will not happen. Valve seats can also be replaced due to wear and tear.

in naturally. This is also known as a 'naturally aspirated' engine, as opposed to a turbo engine (see explanation of turbo later in this chapter).

◆ Stopping a diesel engine

Turning off the ignition key does not always stop a diesel engine; a conventional mechanically fuel-injected diesel engine will run without electrical power at all. We normally have to pull a stop cable, press a stop button or turn the ignition key to a 'stop' position. All of these systems have the same effect, they stop the high-pressure pump sending pressurised fuel to the fuel injector.

An injector works by pressurised fuel entering a nozzle in the end of the injector. This builds up pressure against a needle valve, which is spring loaded. The needle valve is pushed open by the fuel pressure, releasing the fuel into the combustion chamber. So, by not sending any pressurised fuel to the injector, the needle valve will not open and so the engine will immediately stop. A stop cable does this mechanically, a stop button or ignition switch off does this via a solenoid.

If you have a stop cable, don't forget to push it back in once the engine has stopped, otherwise the engine will not start the next time you come to try it.

If, however, your engine does turn off by just returning the ignition key to the 'off' position then it is either a car-derived engine where the 'stop' solenoid needs power to keep the engine running or the engine

is controlled by an 'engine control unit' (ECU) replacing the mechanical fuel system with an electronic system, which injects the fuel more precisely.

How does a four-stroke petrol engine work?

It is exactly the same as a four-stroke diesel with the exception that at the top of the compression stroke the fuel/air mix is ignited by the spark plug, so the strokes are 'Suck, Squeeze and Ignite, Bang, Blow'.

A petrol engine requires a system of distributing the spark across the cylinders. Traditionally, this has been done by a 'distributor', which sends a low voltage signal of engine position or 'points' to the ignition coil which produces a high voltage pulse. This is then sent via a high tension (HT) lead back to the distributor, which then 'distributes' the high voltage pulse to each spark plug in sequence via more HT leads. However, both diesel and petrol engines have become much more sophisticated over time with the introduction of engine management systems or engine control units (ECUs). An engine management system controls the fuel injection and timing electronically and is designed to increase power and economy and reduce emissions. So, a modern petrol engine will normally have an ignition coil directly attached to each spark plug. The ignition coils are turned on and off in sequence via the

HOW A PETROL FOUR-STROKE ENGINE WORKS

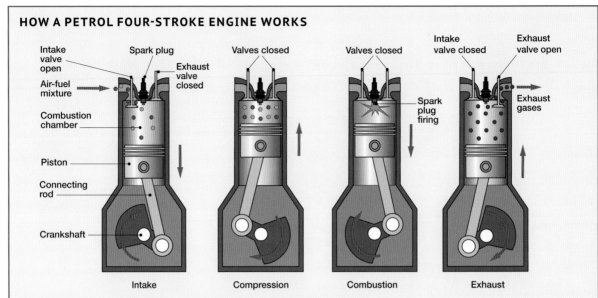

A petrol engine – the pistons are attached to the crankshaft by connecting rods known as 'con rods'. The pistons rise and fall at different times according to where they are attached to the crank.

Four-stroke petrol engine

Stroke	Known as	Piston	Intake valve	Exhaust valve
1. Intake	Suck	Down cylinder, sucks in air and fuel	Open	Closed
2. Compression and spark	Squeeze and ignite	Up cylinder, compresses the air and fuel, which is ignited by a spark	Closed	Closed
3. Combustion	Bang	Down cylinder as fuel and air combust, expanding gases in the cylinder	Closed	Closed
4. Exhaust	Blow	Up cylinder, blowing out the exhaust gases	Closed	Open

engine control unit (ECU) and the engine position is sent to the ECU from a crankshaft position sensor. One of the benefits of an ECU over a traditional distributor system is that there are many fewer components that can wear out (points, distributor, HT leads), so this system needs no maintenance apart from changing the spark plugs.

A petrol engine does not need to be made of such strong and therefore heavy metals as a diesel engine because the combustion of the petrol is not caused entirely by compression but by a spark plug. The air does not need to reach the same temperature as for a diesel engine and so it does not need to be so highly compressed. Therefore, the forces are not so great. In fact, the air in a petrol engine is compressed by 8 to 12 times its original volume, as opposed to the 15 to 22 times required for a diesel engine.

◆ Starting a petrol engine

Turning the ignition key engages the starter motor, which turns over the engine, starts the fuel pumping and starts the electrical process to create a spark from the spark plug. These engines will require electrical power to run.

◆ Increasing the engine speed

Again, like a diesel engine, the more fuel you introduce to the cylinder, the bigger the bang and the greater the power and speed. This is done by introducing a mix of fuel and air blended by a carburettor or injector for fuel and a butterfly valve to introduce varying amounts of air.

This is mixed before being sucked into the cylinders in the 'inlet manifold' ready for the spark plug, which is fitted at the top of the cylinder to ignite the fuel once the air and fuel is fully compressed.

◆ Stopping a petrol engine

Turning off the ignition key simply turns off the power to the electrical ignition system and stops the spark plugs from sparking and the fuel from pumping.

How to hand crank or turn over an engine

Occasionally, you need to check to see if the engine will turn over, especially if you are trying to troubleshoot why the engine won't start. You can turn a diesel engine over by attaching a spanner or wrench to the locking nut of the crankshaft pulley. Turn it clockwise – righty tighty (sorry about that) – and the engine should turn over. It may be that it is very stiff because you are turning the crankshaft and this is pushing the pistons up and down and in so doing you are compressing the air in one or more cylinders. A variety of older diesel engines have a cranking handle so you can turn the engine over by hand and these engines will have 'decompression levers', which will hold open an exhaust valve in each of the cylinders and make turning over the engine by hand easier – there is a decompression lever for each cylinder with a bar linking them so you can release the compression on all cylinders at once. Remember to drop/re-engage etc the decompression lever before trying to start the engine. Of course, if the engine won't turn over then it has probably seized.

An engine control unit (**ECU**) is also referred to as:

engine control module (**ECM**)

powertrain control module (**PCM**)

engine management system (**EMS**)

... which all do exactly the same thing.

WHAT DOES A CRANKSHAFT DO?

A crankshaft converts the vertical motion of the pistons into a rotational motion that drives the prop shaft.

Fuel injector
Inlet camshaft
Exhaust camshaft
Inlet valve
Exhaust valve
Piston
Connecting rod
Crankshaft

A diesel engine cutaway, showing the crankshaft, con rod, piston and valves.

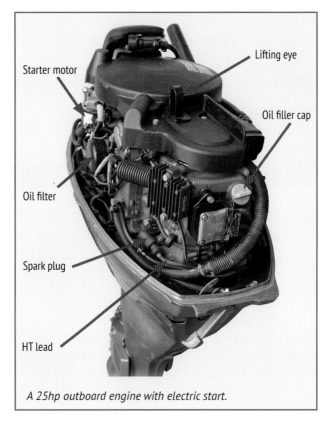

Starter motor
Lifting eye
Oil filler cap
Oil filter
Spark plug
HT lead

A 25hp outboard engine with electric start.

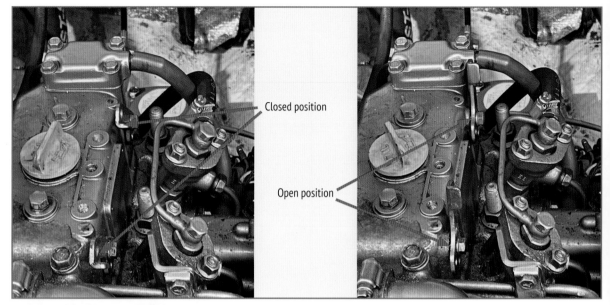

Closed position

Open position

▲ *Yanmar 2GM20 Decompression levers.*

Volvo Penta MD7A. Hand crank handle position.

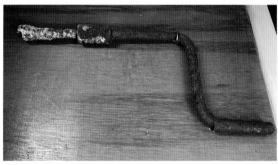

▲ *A crank handle. Given that this is an emergency engine starting device, it would be a good idea to keep it in good condition!*

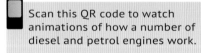 Scan this QR code to watch animations of how a number of diesel and petrol engines work.

Petrol engines do not require the cylinders to be decompressed for you to be able to hand crank the engine as their compression is about half that of a diesel engine. You will still feel the compression but you should always be able to turn the engine over by hand fairly easily.

Turbos and superchargers

What is a turbo or a supercharger actually doing? Essentially, they fool an engine into thinking that it is bigger than it is.

We can tell how big an engine is by the volume in each cylinder. Cylinder volume multiplied by the number of cylinders gives you the size of the engine – 4 cylinders × ½ litre each makes a 2-litre engine.

So, we have ½ a litre of air in each cylinder to compress and that is the maximum amount of air that can be compressed by the piston, unless we blow air under pressure into the cylinder via:

1. A supercharger, which is run off the engine and so uses engine power and which compresses air and blows it into the cylinder.
2. A turbocharger, which is run off the exhaust gases, which power a turbine to compress air and blow it into the cylinder.

If we can now get 1 litre of air into that cylinder under pressure, we have doubled the size of the engine from 2 litres to 4 litres. And because we have doubled the amount of air in the cylinder, we can double the amount of fuel injected and get double the bang and double the power. We don't get exactly double the power but you get the idea.

How the turbine turns the compressor section of the turbo.

There is also a major difference between a turbo and a supercharger and that is that the turbo will only be effective when the air pressure it produces is more than that which the engine can suck in on its own. This air pressure is dictated by the speed of the exhaust exiting through the turbo's turbine, the faster the engine, the more air is produced. So, as the engine starts to rev faster, the turbo effect will kick in at higher revs. Below this is known as turbo lag. Whereas a supercharger run off the engine can be geared and used throughout the rev range.

The diagram above shows how the turbine turns the compressor section of the turbo. But as compressing air causes it to heat up, we need a charge air cooler or intercooler to cool it down; this condenses the air even more before it enters the engine.

How a hybrid setup works

As cars move over to electric motors, so boats will do the same. The only issue being the harvesting, from the sun or the wind, of sufficient electricity to run batteries to power the electric motors. Currently, hybrid arrangements are more popular, where the electricity generation comes from a diesel engine.

Some have the diesel engine and electric motor combined, where either can drive the propeller shaft and you can switch between the two. This is referred to as a parallel system.

Others use a diesel generator to charge the batteries to run the electric motor, which drives the propeller shaft. This is referred to as a series system.

COMMON RAIL DIRECT FUEL INJECTION

You will often hear the term 'common rail technology' being used. This refers to a common rail, which is a long metal cylinder that receives fuel from the fuel pump and provides it to the injectors under extremely high pressure. It is a fairly modern invention and provides power and fuel consumption benefits over older, lower-pressure fuel-injection engines. By injecting the fuel at extremely high pressure, greater than 2,000 bar, a larger number of smaller droplets of fuel are fed into the cylinder. These provide a much higher ratio of surface area to volume, which improves vaporisation. This in turn results in more of the fuel being burnt: in other words, a more complete combustion. The long and short of it is that you get more power and, with less carbon in the exhaust, cleaner emissions.

3 Gearboxes and drives

The type of vessel determines the best propulsion system for it.

Shaft and propeller

The most basic and traditional type for an engine is a propeller on a shaft. It is a simple design using a basic gearbox with forward and reverse and the gearbox is normally bolted on to the back of the engine, aft of the engine. Attached to that is a coupling, which then attaches to the shaft. The shaft then goes through the stern tube set in the hull of the boat and some sort of seal is used, either a stuffing box, lip seal or face seal, to allow the shaft to turn in the tube and yet prevent water from entering the boat.

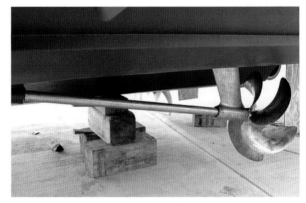

▲ *Shaft drive and propeller.*

The propeller will be fitted on to the end of the shaft. There may be a keyway in the shaft and the propeller to prevent it slipping on the shaft. A keyway is a slot cut in the shaft and the propeller into which a rectangle of metal plate slots and is held in place by the propeller once fitted.

Having a keyway also reduces the chance of the nut on the end of the propeller coming loose as there is much less movement of the propeller as it moves from forward to reverse gear than if there was no keyway.

The shaft itself may be held in position by the addition of either a cutlass bearing, which is fitted into the hull at the exit point of the shaft, or it may also be suspended on what we call a 'P' bracket, which supports the shaft and houses a cutlass bearing within it.

A 'P' bracket allows you to have a longer shaft. This is important when it comes to getting the propeller closer

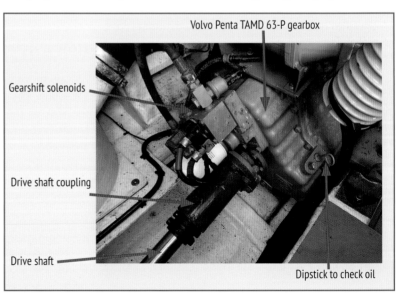

Volvo Penta TAMD 63-P gearbox

Gearshift solenoids

Drive shaft coupling

Drive shaft

Dipstick to check oil

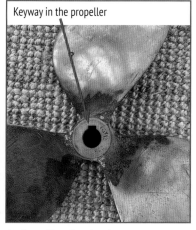

Keyway in the propeller

P-bracket (shaft removed)

Cutlass bearing in P-bracket

▲ *Propeller showing keyway.*

▲ *P-bracket and cutlass bearing inside.*

to the rudder, which allows you to throw more water off the rudder and thus make the rudder more responsive under engine.

You will find gearbox and shaft propeller systems on both sailing boats and motorboats, but a note about steerage:

- Motorboats generally go faster than sailing boats and so do not need a large rudder to deflect sufficient water to be able to give them steerage.
- Sailing boats heel a great deal more and need a large rudder to deflect enough water when the angle of the rudder is no longer perpendicular, especially as they are also travelling relatively slowly through the water by comparison with most motorboats.

The rudder on a sailing boat becomes less efficient the more it heels

To overcome this, designers have introduced twin rudders, but what you gain on the swings you lose on the roundabouts as this can make close-quarter handling trickier. Generally you need a bit more speed than with a single rudder to get a flow of water over the rudders that are angled away from the perpendicular to get the best out of them.

When perpendicular, the rudder is very efficient at deflecting water left or right to provide steerage.

As the boat heels, the rudder starts deflecting water not so much left and right as partially up and down and so becomes less efficient.

▼ *Twin rudders on a sailing boat.*

As a consequence of having small rudders, motorboats do not derive much steerage from the rudders in slow speed close-quarters manoeuvres or when going astern. If a motorboat has twin engines, then it is these working individually or in opposition that will be used when close-quarter manoeuvring, or of course bow and stern thrusters, which you will also find on some sailing boats.

STERN GLANDS – STUFFING BOXES, LIP SEALS AND FACE SEALS

All three stern glands fit over the stern tube where it enters the hull and within which a seal is attached that fits round the propeller shaft. And all three are designed to stop sea water invading the boat.

Stuffing boxes form a seal between the end of the stern tube and the propeller shaft, which prevents water from entering the boat and yet allows the shaft to spin. Rings of flax packing are compressed around the shaft by the tightening of a nut to create the seal. There will always be a small leak of water through a stuffing box, which allows for cooling and lubrication. A maximum of one drip every 20 seconds is about right while running but it should only drip occasionally if at all when stationary. Anything more than this needs to be investigated. Either the nut needs tightening or the packing material needs to be replaced. When replacing packing material, remember:

1. That the stern tube is below the waterline – does the boat need to be lifted for this?
2. To monitor the drip rate with the new packing and adjust the compression of the nut accordingly. Over-tightening the stuffing box will result in restricting the movement of the shaft, which we need to avoid, so a balance needs to be achieved. Due to wear and tear to the packing material, stuffing boxes need to be checked regularly and adjustments made when required.

Face seals compress a carbon bearing against a collar, which is attached to the shaft and a hose connects the fixed bearing to the stern tube. Lubrication is by a film of water between the metal shaft and the carbon. These are dripless seals.

Lip seals are similar to face seals except that instead of two faces being compressed against each other in the case of the face seal, with the lip seal a spring compresses a rubber ring against the shaft. Again, lip seal stern glands are designed to be drip-free. If you do notice a drip then the lip seal will need to be replaced. Generally, manufacturers will recommend that these types of

The parts of a stuffing box

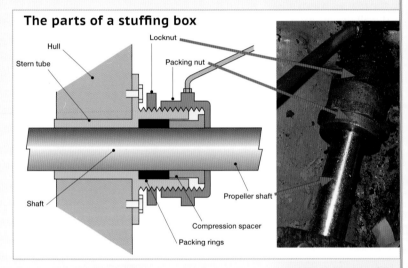

Hull
Stern tube
Locknut
Packing nut
Shaft
Propeller shaft
Compression spacer
Packing rings

Face seal

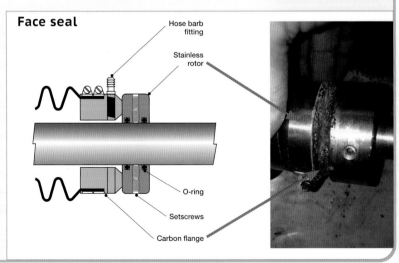

Hose barb fitting
Stainless rotor
O-ring
Setscrews
Carbon flange

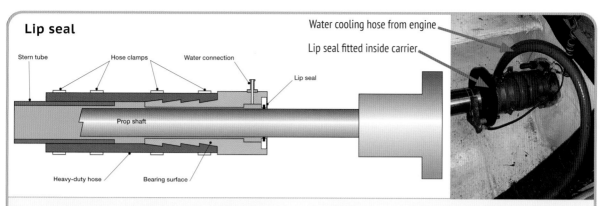

Lip seal

Stern tube

Hose clamps

Water connection

Lip seal

Prop shaft

Heavy-duty hose

Bearing surface

Water cooling hose from engine

Lip seal fitted inside carrier

seals are replaced every five years. Where room and design allow, engineers can fit a spare lip seal to the shaft so replacement can be done in an emergency with the boat in the water or during an emergency lift, without the need to disconnect the shaft. Lip seal stern glands must be water lubricated and cannot be allowed to dry. If they do, the seal will become damaged very quickly.

All stern glands require water lubrication. In the case of stuffing boxes, seepage up the stern tube and a drip rate of a maximum of once every 20 seconds is sufficient. Smaller displacement boats will also usually have a grease tube attached to a remote grease pump so grease can be pressured into the packing to help seal and lubricate. On larger high-speed boats, the packing is greased when fitted and then pressurised water from the engine is forced into the stern tube to help lubricate and cool the shaft where grease

alone is not enough to keep temperatures down.

In the case of face seals and some lip seals, a pressured source of cooling water is required and this is fed off the raw-water system from the engine and pumped to the stern gland.

In the case of twin-engine boats, there could be an occasion where one engine may fail and it might be necessary to run under one engine alone. In this case, the failed engine would not be sending any cooling water to the stern gland. The propeller would be turning the shaft, which may overheat, break the lip seal and allow sea water to enter the boat up the stern tube. The answer to this is either to have both engines feed cooling water to both stern glands, or to have a switchable crossover system. This is particularly important where the drive is from a hydraulic gearbox (found on larger engines) where it may not be possible to lock off the propeller shaft.

Spare packing cut to size in case of leak requiring emergency replacement

Stern tube. This type has a cutlass bearing inside

Compression ring, to compress the packing material

Water cooling pipe from engine

Carbon brushes to electrically connect the shaft and prop to the anodes, rudder and P-bracket to reduce galvanic corrosion

Adjust tightness of compression ring by tightening these nuts to stop leaks but not too much to restrict the turning of the shaft

Pressurised water is pumped from the engine into the stuffing box behind the packing to help cool the shaft. This water exits through the seaward end of the stern gland and should not affect the drip rate of no more than one drip every 20 seconds.

Sail drive

This is fitted through the hull, generally just behind the keel, with the propeller further forward than on a shaft system. It has a gearbox mounted on the back of the engine but instead of this attaching to a shaft, the gearbox itself actually drops down under the boat and so the bottom half of the gearbox is underwater and from this is a very short shaft just long enough to attach the propeller.

A sail drive causes less drag than a conventional shaft system, especially if the shaft system has a 'P' bracket. Sail drives will be found on racing sailing boats or racer-cruisers. Sail drives are mainly fitted to sailing boats.

▲ Sail drive.

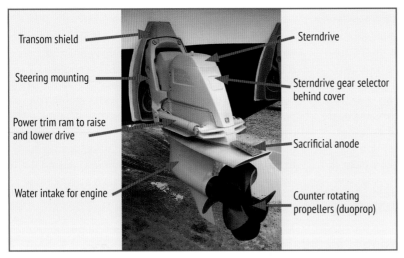

Transom shield

Steering mounting

Power trim ram to raise and lower drive

Water intake for engine

Sterndrive

Sterndrive gear selector behind cover

Sacrificial anode

Counter rotating propellers (duoprop)

▲ A transom shield is the connection between the sterndrive and the engine, with the engine bolted to it on one side and the sterndrive on the other side.

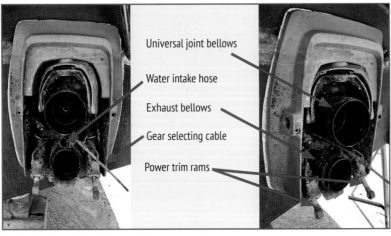

Universal joint bellows

Water intake hose

Exhaust bellows

Gear selecting cable

Power trim rams

▲ Transom shield with sterndrive removed.

Because the propeller is some distance from the rudder on a sail drive, the rudder tends to be wider than normal. This also helps when going astern as you get directional control more quickly at slow speeds than with a shaft system. Added to which a sail drive will create less prop walk than a shaft drive system.

The exhaust exits the boat through the side of the hull.

Sterndrive

A sterndrive, also referred to as an outdrive or a 'Z' drive because of its 'Z' shape, is a propulsion and steering system in one. The sterndrive itself moves to steer the boat, like a rudder. It is attached to the back of a motorboat engine and so the engine has to be right at the stern of the boat.

A shaft from the engine goes through a transom shield and into the gearbox of the sterndrive. The transom shield protects both engine and sterndrive from water ingress.

Like a sail drive, the gearbox in a sterndrive is under water. Unlike a sail drive, the exhaust does not exit through the side hull but usually through the transom shield at the stern.

There being no need for a rudder on a sterndrive boat, the boat is very easy to steer astern. You point the sterndrive where you want the boat to go and that's it.

You can also lift a sterndrive up so it is level with the hull and although you can't run the engine when it is like this, it does mean that you can beach the boat. You can also put the boat on a trailer with the sterndrive lifted.

And you can use the sterndrive to raise or lower the bow to match the sea conditions by 'trimming' the drive slightly up or down, which changes the vertical angle of the propeller, forcing the bow of the boat to nose either down or up to get her running smoothly and at optimal efficiency.

A standard shaft-driven boat will use trim tabs for this. That said, a sterndrive boat will also have trim tabs, which are adjusted to keep her level in a sea, or crosswind. And because you can only trim a sterndrive to a certain degree to get the bow down, a trim tab is used to get the bow down further.

Trim tabs on shaft-driven boats and sterndrives are also used when you want to remain on the plane but at a slower speed. Say you want to remain on the plane at 18 knots, which is probably on the edge for most boats between running in semi-displacement mode and planing, then if you trim the tabs down this will lift the stern out of the water and the boat may well remain on the plane.

Another advantage of a sterndrive over a shaft drive, beyond the fact that you can steer the boat with them, which gives you a much more immediate response, and that you can trim the boat with them, is that they are aqua-dynamically shaped and create less drag compared to a shaft and a 'P' bracket.

Twin sterndrives can be operated independently in terms of gears, both forward, both astern or one forward and the other astern, and in terms of trim, but traditionally in terms of steering they are coupled together. When you turn the helm, both drives turn the same amount. The same applies if you have three sterndrives.

However, newer electronic systems allow the sterndrives to be operated in a truly independent way and when manoeuvring at low speeds a joystick

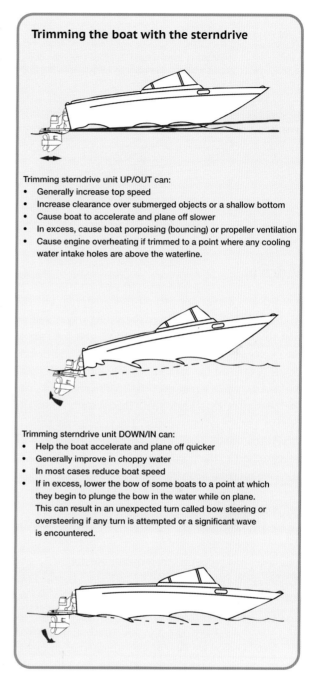

Trimming the boat with the sterndrive

Trimming sterndrive unit UP/OUT can:
- Generally increase top speed
- Increase clearance over submerged objects or a shallow bottom
- Cause boat to accelerate and plane off slower
- In excess, cause boat porpoising (bouncing) or propeller ventilation
- Cause engine overheating if trimmed to a point where any cooling water intake holes are above the waterline.

Trimming sterndrive unit DOWN/IN can:
- Help the boat accelerate and plane off quicker
- Generally improve in choppy water
- In most cases reduce boat speed
- If in excess, lower the bow of some boats to a point at which they begin to plunge the bow in the water while on plane. This can result in an unexpected turn called bow steering or oversteering if any turn is attempted or a significant wave is encountered.

is used instead of the helm. Point the joystick where you want the boat to go and the engines will take you there – whether that be ahead, astern or sideways – 360 degree control. Mercury have a 360 degree system called Zeus. Obviously, these systems require a twin sterndrive setup.

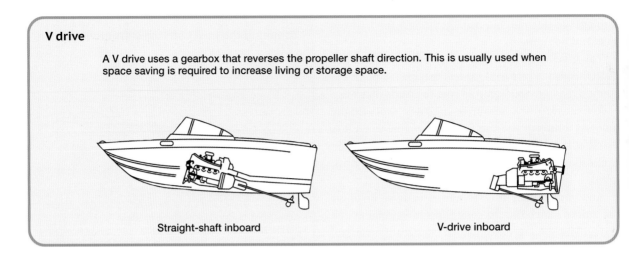

V drive

A V drive uses a gearbox that reverses the propeller shaft direction. This is usually used when space saving is required to increase living or storage space.

Straight-shaft inboard   V-drive inboard

V drive

A V drive is essentially a shaft-driven system but the engine inside the boat is fitted the wrong way round, so that the front of the engine points aft and the rear of the engine points forward. The gearbox is now obviously pointing forward but is designed for the shaft to point backwards, which goes under the engine and then exits the boat through a shaft seal. This system is usually used as a space saving exercise. The engines on a shaft-driven boat would normally be positioned amidships. By using a V drive, the engines can be placed at the stern, allowing room for an extra cabin to be fitted amidships.

Pod systems

A pod system uses two or more engines that drive gearboxes and propellers underneath the hull.

The system was developed by Volvo and is called the Integrated Propulsion System (IPS).

Here, the propellers face forward rather than aft and they normally have two counter-rotating propellers attached, known as duo props, where one propeller rotates one way and the second propeller rotates the other way.

With the propellers facing forward when you put the gear into ahead, the wash is sent aft and so the propellers are always turning in clean water. With a conventional shaft propulsion, the propeller is turning in disturbed water that has come off the keel, the P-bracket and the shaft. The same applies to a sterndrive where the water flows round the front of the sterndrive before

the propeller can get a grip on it. As a result, pod drives are more efficient. And of course, the design of the pods allows them to turn through a greater arc than a sterndrive, which can only turn between 90° and 100°, allowing for better manoeuvrability with pods over any other propulsion system at low speeds.

A couple of things to remember about pods:

1. Being fixed under the hull, they increase the draught or clearance of the boat. They tend to hang down lower than a sterndrive or shaft drive and so require more water in which to float the boat. The net result is that you have to be careful of grounding or hitting a submerged object, such as a rock. Also, while they do have a 'weak' point so that they will snap off if they hit something, were they not to snap off but to tear a hole in the hull of the boat, well, enough said. Calibrating your depth sounder carefully and

▲ *A pod system.*

allowing a sensible margin of error is important for boats with pods. On the upside, experience has shown that if a boat with pods is run aground gently into mud or sand then the pods do not appear to break off and, having waited for the tide to come up, the boat can be towed back into port.

2. The second thing to consider with pods is the effect of wind on the bow. Pods are highly manoeuvrable in close quarters. With the Volvo IPS system you point the stick where you want the boat to go and that is where it goes. Out on the high seas, it is asking a lot of pods fitted towards the stern to be able to hold the bow up to the wind. The high freeboard of a motorboat presents itself to the wind just as a sail would on a sailing boat. And so, despite the claims of the salesperson that an IPS system can handle anything, do have a bow thruster fitted. We were trying to drive a Sealine F42 with pods and no bow thruster into the tide and wind towards a mooring buoy and the wind would just catch the bow and blow it off and there was nothing we could do with the pods to prevent this. We needed a bow thruster to help. As it was, we turned the boat round, presented the stern of the boat to the wind, drove astern up to the buoy and picked it up from the stern.

Note: If you hear the term Azipod, this refers to a system developed by ABB and is an electric motor geared to a propeller, just like a pod, except that the complete Azipod is outside the hull, whereas a pod has the diesel engine inside the hull and the gearbox and shaft in the pod outside the hull.

COUNTER-ROTATING PROPELLERS

These require two shafts, one inside the other. The outer shaft is shorter than the inner and has one propeller fixed to it and the inner shaft is longer and has the other propeller fixed to it. The gearbox then drives the two shafts in opposite directions. The vertical shaft in the gearbox has a gear on the end, one of the duo prop shafts gears to one side of it and the other shaft gears to the other side. Thus, when the vertical shaft turns, one shaft will turn anticlockwise while the other will turn clockwise and so the propellers counter-rotate. The benefit of this is that the lateral effect of the propellers is cancelled out and the boat is stabilised.

Where you have one propeller on a shaft in a high-performance boat the lateral effect of the propeller will tend to lean the boat over in one direction and will require the use of trim tabs to level up the boat.

Counter rotating propellers also allow you to increase thrust from the engine by having two propellers without added 'lean'.

Here the propeller is a right-handed propeller, which turns clockwise when in ahead, and it is leaning the boat to starboard. It would require trim tabs to right the boat until she was level.

Here we have a duo prop on a sterndrive. This is a counter-rotating propeller and while one propeller is right-handed and turning clockwise in ahead and would try to make the boat lean to starboard, the other propeller, also right-handed, is spinning in the opposite direction, trying to lean the boat to port. The two propellers cancel each other out, so the boat is level.

Other drives

The most common drives are described above, but there are others, such as:

◆ Surface drive

Here, the shaft comes out through the transom of the boat as opposed to through the hull below, so the propeller is half in and out of the water. The result of this is that the propeller throws water up into the air in what is referred to as a 'rooster tail', because of the shape it creates. The idea of the surface drive is that because the shaft exits the boat through the transom,

▲ *Rooster tail – thank you to Diane Ward for this photo.*

it reduces drag – by comparison with a standard shaft system or a sterndrive. You can also angle the shaft of the surface drive up or down and so you can trim the boat much like you can with a sterndrive. Surface-drive systems tend to be seen on very high-performance planing 'V' hulled boats and catamarans. They are also seen on Pershing and Mangusta performance motor cruisers. The propellers, being close to the surface of the water, are potentially dangerous, which is why makers of pleasure craft add a bathing platform, which is attached to the stern of the boat and provides protection from the drives and propellers.

▲ *Notice how close to the surface of the water the propellers are.*

Some surface-drive systems are used to steer the boat, similar to a sterndrive, only with a smaller amount of directional movement. Others use fixed shafts and a rudder.

Close-quarter manoeuvring is difficult with this type of propulsion system, which is why it is found mostly on racing boats. But where it is used on pleasure motor cruisers they will also be fitted with bow and stern thrusters.

◆ Jet drive

Jet drives work by sucking in water underneath the boat and then blowing it out of the back, through a nozzle at high pressure.

Jetskis use jet drives, as do some RIBs and motorboats. One advantage is that they can go into shallow waters. So, rescue boats often have jet drives. Steering is managed by turning the nozzle at the stern left and right. Jet drives only have forward gear – they always have to suck in water and blow it out the back. So to go astern, much like the reverse-thrust system on an aeroplane, a cowl – known as a 'bucket' – comes down over the end of the nozzle to direct the thrust forward.

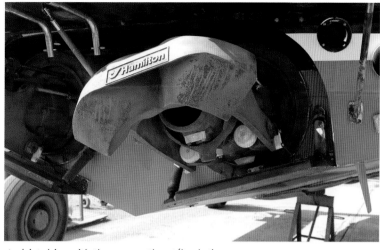

▲ A jet drive with the reverse thrust 'bucket'.

▲ Jetski with 'pee hole' indicating that raw water is flowing through the cooling system.

◆ Outboard engines

Outboards attach to the transom of the boat and are self-contained. Newer and more high-performance engines now have duo prop systems (two counter-rotating propellers). The benefit here is that they are able to produce great power without introducing 'lean'. Single-propeller outboards will encourage the boat to 'lean', which on larger, more powerful RIBs and motorboats you can 'trim' out with trim tabs.

Outboards can also be trimmed up and down, according to the sea state, to achieve the best ride and the maximum efficiency. And of course, you can trim the outboard right up out of the water when not in use, to protect it from the effects of the water and marine growth.

Propeller pitch

Pitch is the angle the blades of the propeller make when cutting through the water and is dictated by the engine, the gearbox and the speed you want to go, or rather the speed your boat is capable of going. Displacement boats will only ever go at displacement speed – see the formula below for working this out.

These factors also determine where you want your power. At low speed? Or at high speed?

A propeller with blades that are angled out – fine pitch – so quite flat in appearance will have very high low-speed power but will not drive the boat very fast.

The more you angle the blades outwards – coarse pitch – the faster the boat will go but the less power it will have at low speeds.

PROP WALK

Prop walk, the effect of the boat moving sideways, is caused by two things:

1. The effect of the turning propeller pulling the boat in a certain direction.
2. The effect of prop wash along the hull of the boat. In ahead, this wash is sent towards the rudder and the rudder is then used to steer the boat. But in astern this wash is sent down the hull and can physically move the boat to one side or another.

You get prop walk in both ahead and in astern from a single propeller, although it is much more noticeable in astern than ahead, because in ahead the propeller wash flows over the rudder giving almost instant steerage even at very slow speeds. In astern, it takes much longer for the rudder to have any appreciable effect as there is now no propeller wash over it, and so there is more time when prop walk is affecting the boat before the rudder comes into play.

Knowing which way your boat 'kicks' in astern is extremely important and becomes part of your close-quarter strategy when manoeuvring.

If you don't know which way it kicks, click the

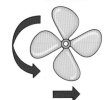
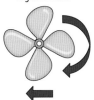

Left-handed	Right-handed
Rotates anticlockwise as you look at it from the stern. Prop walk in astern to starboard. Slight prop walk to port in ahead.	Rotates clockwise as you look at it from the stern. Prop walk in astern to port. Slight prop walk to starboard in ahead.

▲ *How right-handed and left-handed propellers affect prop walk in astern and ahead.*

boat into astern when tied to the dock. If there is turbulence on one side of the boat and clear water on the other side, she will kick in the direction of the clear water. If there is a little turbulence on either side then she may well have no appreciable kick in either direction. Kick depends on hull shape and propulsion system.

Yachts with single engines therefore experience prop walk from slight for a boat with a sail drive to considerable for a long-keel boat with a propeller inset into the rudder. It gets worse for traditional long-keel sailing boats with an offset propeller!

Prop wash in astern

Bow

Stern

▲ *Before the test – water calm.*

▲ *Engine astern creating turbulence (prop wash) on port, which will move the stern of the boat to starboard.*

Motorboat drive options comparison

Drive type	Price	Servicing cost	Efficiency	Manoeuvrability
Shaft	2	1	6	5
Stern	3	3	3	2
Jet	4	4	5	4
Pod	6	6	4	1
Surface	5	5	2	6
Outboard	1	2	1	3

Code: 1 = cheapest to buy, to service, most efficient, most manoeuvrable
6 = most expensive to buy, to service, least efficient, least manoeuvrable

It is very important to have the pitch of the propeller matched to the gearbox and the power or rev range of the engine. It is no good fitting a propeller with too coarse a pitch. If you have an engine that is designed to run at a maximum of 6,000rpm and you fit a propeller that is too coarse a pitch, you may find that the engine will only run at a maximum of 5,000rpm, for example.

So, in terms of propeller size and pitch, a balance must always be struck because different types of boat doing different things have different requirements.

A speedboat for waterskiing will want a fine propeller to allow you to get speed up quickly. However, a fine pitch propeller may mean you sacrifice top speed because while you will get the maximum revs out of the engine, the fine pitch of the propeller will not drive you as fast through the water as the engine is capable.

WHAT IS PROPELLER PITCH?

A coarse pitched propeller travels further through the water in one revolution than a fine pitched propeller.

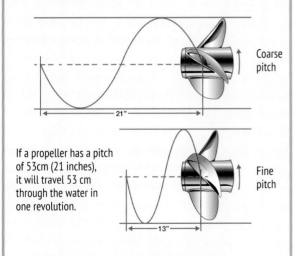

Coarse pitch

21"

If a propeller has a pitch of 53cm (21 inches), it will travel 53 cm through the water in one revolution.

Fine pitch

13"

So in relation to the engine and gearbox, the pitch of the propeller determines the speed of the boat when on the plane.

DO WE LOCK THE PROP OR LET IT SPIN WHEN SAILING?

This is a debate that comes up in the yachting magazines from time to time.

The answer is that in terms of efficiency the boat will sail faster if the propeller is allowed to spin. But that is not the end of the issue. Actually that is just the start, because while some gearboxes are happy spinning without the engine running, other gearboxes actually need the engine to be running to keep them cool as they have their own heat exchangers. So you must not allow the propeller to spin. You need to check to see if your gearbox has its own heat exchanger. This is likely to be the case on large yachts.

And if the propeller shaft is cooled by raw water fed from the engine, then allowing it to spin with the engine off will overheat the shaft, damage the shaft seal and you will end up with sea water leaking into the boat.

There are of course folding and feathering propellers that allow you to reduce drag while locking the shaft.

Refer to the manual for advice.

▲ *A single engine Nordhavn with wing engine and wing shaft offset – a spare to get you home if the main engine fails.*

▲ *Propeller and rudder protected by a special coating to prevent marine growth.*

A planing motorboat will want a propeller that is balanced between fine and coarse pitch to allow it to get onto the plane as quickly as possible and yet reach a decent top speed.

Bow and stern thrusters

These are available as the standard through-hull propeller type, or as jet thrusters. The advantage of jet thrusters over propeller thrusters is that they are much quieter, pretty much silent, there is no propeller to foul, they can be fitted more or less anywhere on the boat, so can be set at the extremities for greater effect, and are easy to instal.

◆ A couple of things to note if the thruster stops working

First of all, if a thruster is going to stop working it will do so while you are using it. So before use, you need it check that it is working. This way you can put a plan B into operation in plenty of time.

Thruster motors have a shear pin, which will break off if there is any major resistance from the propeller, perhaps if some detritus has got past the wire guards protecting the tunnel and jammed the propeller. In this case, pressing

▲ Bow thruster.　　▼ Stern thruster.

the thruster button will result in a high-pitched whine of the motor and no movement as the propeller will have been disconnected. Spare shear pins are usually attached to the motor and can be changed while afloat – assuming you have checked that the propeller is free to spin.

Do make sure you know where the thruster 'trip fuse' is located. This will be near the battery. Prior to the shear pin breaking, it may be that the thruster under strain will trip the fuse, which will result in all power being lost to the thruster.

Do make sure that the battery is switched on and is connected, of course.

◆ Bow thrusting

A word about bow thrusting. Most people put the bow thruster on for a burst of about 1 second at a time, fearful that the thruster will overheat with overuse.

Vetus told us that if you held it in for TWO and a HALF minutes solidly you might want to allow it to cool down for an hour before using it again. So don't worry about overheating your thrusters.

Modes of travel

The way your boat moves through the water and its maximum speed depends on hull design.

◆ Displacement hull

A displacement hull is designed to drive through the water and will have a maximum speed attainable that is directly related to the length along the waterline.

This is called the hull speed and can be calculated for any given boat. It is 1.34 x the $\sqrt{}$ length along the waterline (LWL) in feet. This formula, known as the speed to length ratio (SLR), refers to the distance between the bow and stern wave crests – one wavelength. If working in metres it is 2.43 x the $\sqrt{}$ LWL = hull speed.

A boat with length overall (LOA) of 40 feet and a length along the waterline (LWL) of 35 feet will have a maximum hull speed in displacement mode of

$$\sqrt{35} = 5.92 \times 1.34 = 8 \text{ knots}$$

As a boat goes faster than her hull speed, she starts to climb the bow wave. At the same time, her stern sinks down into the trough in the water, caused by her forward movement.

▲ Displacement hull.

▲ Climbing the bow wave, the stern of this boat is sinking into the trough. She is going faster than her hull speed.

▲ Semi-displacement, she is climbing the bow wave ahead and is straddling two waves.

▲ A boat on the plane.

◆ Semi-displacement

A semi-displacement hull is designed to lift out of the water and on top of the bow wave and with added 'lift' aft to counter the stern sinking. She will be able to travel faster than a displacement-hulled boat.

How much faster does very much depend on hull design and the power of the engines but a rough guide for a 40-foot LOA boat with an LWL of 35 feet would be between 1.5 and 2.5 times faster (1.5 x 8 = 12 knots, 2.5 x 8 = 20 knots).

◆ Planing

A planing hull is designed to climb out of the water and to 'hydro-plane', hence 'planing'. It takes a lot more power to climb over the bow wave and get the boat out of the water than it does to maintain the boat on the plane.

On the plane there is less wetted area and less resistance.

Displacement and semi-displacement boats will have smaller engines than a planing boat because it takes an enormous amount of power to get the boat over the bow wave and up on to the plane.

A planing boat will quickly climb the bow wave and get up on the plane. Generally, they start to plane at around the top end of the semi-displacement hull speeds, roughly 18 knots, revs about 2,500. In terms of efficiency, though, it is important to increase revs so the boat is well on the plane, because if you stay at the speed she requires to get up on to the plane you will have to adjust the trim tabs to raise the stern and so will increase drag and increase fuel consumption. Planing at between 3,000 and 3,500 revs is generally the most economic.

Going flat out increases fuel consumption enormously. It is generally considered that a boat will use twice as much fuel flat out on the plane as she will when just on the plane at 2,500 revs and as we have said at the 2,500 revs level this is not especially fuel efficient.

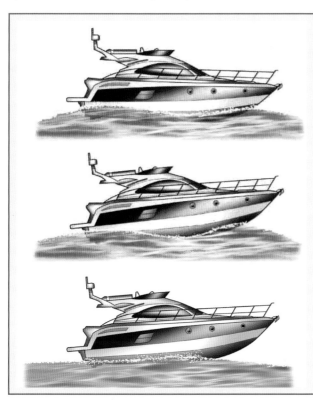

Displacement
Crest of bow and stern wave
= length of waterline
= max hull speed
= economic

Semi-displacement
Bow climbing wave
Stern dropped into trough of wave
= uneconomic

Planing
Hull mostly out of water
Very little wetted area
More economic than climbing the bow wave

Fuel consumption (1 = most efficient, 5 = least efficient)

Mode	Type of hull design		
	Displacement	Semi-displacement	Planing
Hull speed	1	1	1
Climbing the bow wave – semi-displacement	n/a	4	4
Just up on the plane	n/a	n/a	3
Planing, cruising speed	n/a	n/a	2
Flat out	5	5	5

And here are the stats for a Bavaria 32 planing boat, that support this:

	Speed	Fuel consumption
Displacement	7 knots	9.3lph; 0.75 nautical miles/litre
Semi-displacement	9.4 knots	24.3lph; 0.39 nm/litre
Planing	22.2 knots	38.1lph; 0.58nm/litre
Flat out	32.8 knots	87.5lph; 0.37 nm/litre

▲ *A Princess 52 Flybridge at displacement speed.*

Jonathan says

A 55-foot Sunseeker in Yarmouth, Isle of Wight was taking on water. They had the bilge pumps running but the bilge pumps weren't coping.

As I got into Yarmouth, I saw the boat with all the harbourmaster dories around it. There was a big pipe coming out the side, with water gushing out of it. I soon came to realise that it was not just the bilge pumps that were not coping with the water coming in, it was the petrol-powered bilge pump that the harbour master had put in the boat as well as the bilge pumps on the Sunseeker that were just about keeping this thing afloat … just about.

But they didn't know where the water was coming from. So the first thing I had to do was jump on board and find out. It appeared to be coming from the engine bay but where was it getting in? Hard to say, given that the level of water in there was up to my knees already.

We also have electric pumps on the RIB and they are quite powerful at 3,000lph, so I put one of those on as well and the level gradually started to come down. As the level fell, we could see the water coming in through the shaft seal of both shafts – the boat was a shaft drive.

I was told the boat had just gone in the water in Lymington, about 2 miles away, and that they had driven it over to Yarmouth straight away. Shortly after setting off, the bilge alarms had started going. The engines seemed to be working fine.

I had a look at the starboard engine propeller shaft seal. This is fed with cooling raw water from the engine via a 10mm diameter pipe, which attaches to the side of the shaft seal housing.

However, the pipe had broken off, which meant that the shaft seal had been starved of cooling water and had therefore become hot. So hot in fact that it had destroyed the rubber lip seal that's designed to prevent any water from entering the boat. While the boat was underway, the motion of the boat through the water and the resulting 'suction effect' had prevented any significant amount of sea water from coming up the shaft, past the broken lip seal and into the boat. Nonetheless, the starboard engine had been pumping cooling water through this broken pipe and that was flooding into the engine bay. But the minute the boat had slowed and then moored and the engines switched off, while no cooling water was now being pumped by the engine, sea water was, however, rushing up the shaft through the lip seal.

To make matters worse the port shaft seal was leaking, despite the fact that the raw-water cooling hose was connected correctly to the shaft seal. This shaft seal would have been cooled by raw water pumped through it by the port engine. So why was the shaft seal leaking?

After checking the system I came to realise there was a pipe with a shut-off valve fitted that links both port and starboard shaft seals together and the valve was open. You only open the valve on a twin-engine boat if you have an engine failure. This allows cooling water that is being fed by the functioning engine to pass also into the shaft seal of the failed engine, to cool the propeller shaft, which will still be turning, because of the flow of sea water over the propeller as the boat travels through the water.

Both shafts had overheated. The starboard shaft seal wasn't getting any cooling water because of the broken pipe. The port engine was getting less cooling water than it required because with the valve being open the water was following the path of least resistance and heading across to the starboard shaft seal and straight out of the end of the broken pipe.

So during the crossing, the boat had been filling up with water from both the port engine cooling system and the starboard engine cooling system. If the shut-off valve had been shut the port engine would have been isolated from the incident, its shaft seal would have been cooled and it wouldn't have pumped water into the boat.

The boat had V drives, where the engines are the opposite way round to a standard installation.

As a result the stern glands were under each engine, making access very difficult indeed. I had to get under the engines to fix things and don't forget that water was still pouring in. The only way I could do it was to take two jubilee clips and tie them together and get them round the rubber sleeve of the port stern gland and tighten them up to close the rubber sleeve on to the shaft, and I could only get one hand into the space. Still, I managed to join the two jubilee clips together one-handed, get them round the shaft and tighten them enough with one hand to get a tool on to them to tighten them fully. This locked the sleeve to the shaft and reduced the water ingress. Now the shaft could not be turned as this would have damaged the stern gland further but the leak was now down to a trickle.

This then allowed me to undo the stern gland housing to release the damaged rubber seal, cut it off and replace it.

Usually you find a spare lip seal conveniently stored on the shaft for just such a situation, and luckily for me, that was the case here. At the same time I had to block off the hole left from the hose being broken off and turn off the shut-off valve to the other engine.

Of course, lifting the boat would have been a good idea but the only place with a hoist big enough was back in Lymington.

We thought about towing the boat back to Lymington with just the stern gland rubber sleeve tightened with the jubilee clips, but if we had done that there would have been the possibility that with the propellers turning, as they would with the boat being towed through the water, this would put further strain on the stern glands and could have ripped them apart, which would have made the problem worse.

There was the option to tow the boat with both engines in gear to lock off the propellers but first of all the gearboxes were hydraulic and might not have stopped the propellers from turning and worse still there was every chance that the pressure of the water on the propellers with the boat being towed might get them turning and start the engines – in effect bump-starting the engines. In any event, as the spare lip seals were handy it made sense to fit them.

So, once I had managed to replace the seals on both shafts, we were in a position to tow the boat slowly back to Lymington – keeping a sharp eye on the seals – and into a waiting lifting dock ready to hoist.

Moral of the story: when you launch a boat check for leaks, listen for the sound of trickling water, have a look in the engine room once the engines have been started and sort the problem before being released from the slings.

4 Fuel systems

It goes without saying that you need to deliver your engine the best quality fuel you can with no contaminants, debris, water or air in it.

So you need to get to know your fuel system and keep on top of your fuel quality.

How the fuel system works

Fuel is sucked up from the fuel tank by a mechanical or electric fuel lift pump to the engine and pumped round the system at around 1 bar of pressure.

Below is a diagram of a diesel fuel system showing the parts of the system under pressure – within the green dotted line – and the parts that are not.

Fuel pre-filter and water separators are fitted to 90 per cent of boats and have a drain on the bottom to release any water that has gathered there. Water, being heavier than diesel or petrol, will settle at the bottom of the water separator. If you can't see a pre-filter and water separator, it may be that the on-engine filter has a water separator element to it. Check with the engine manufacturer. It is always a good idea to have a separate pre-filter and water separator to prevent water that has not been removed from the fuel from damaging the fuel pumps and injectors and corroding the internal parts of the engine.

Diesel circulating around the system acts as a lubricant for the injection pump and the fuel injector so much more diesel is supplied to the engine than required to run. Excess diesel will find its way back to

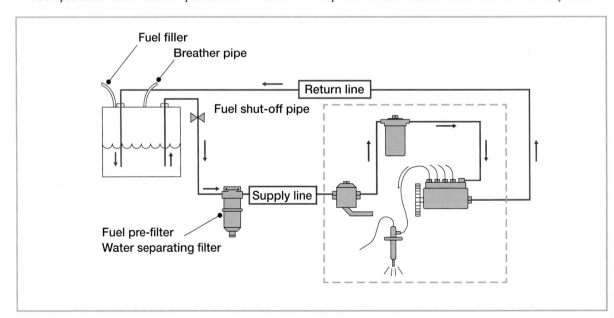

▲ *The fuel system showing the unpressurised side of the system from the tank to the fuel pre-filter and water separator.*

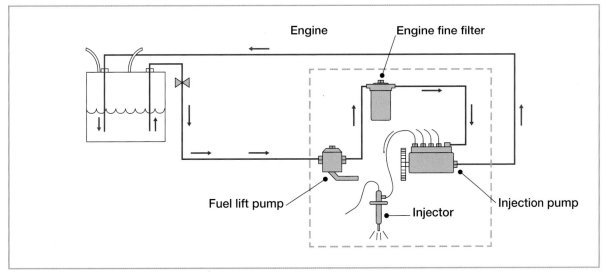

▲ *The fuel system showing the pressurised side of the system in the green box, being the lift pump, the on-engine fuel filter, the injection pump and the injectors and the blue line for excess diesel returning to the fuel tank.*

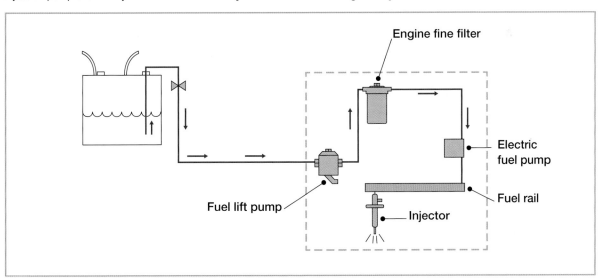

▲ *The fuel system showing the pressurised side of the system in the green box, being the lift pump, the on-engine fuel filter, the electric fuel pump, fuel rail and the injectors.*

the fuel tank in most systems as shown above – the blue line – but systems can differ and take excess diesel back to the fuel filter instead to go around the system again.

Above is a petrol fuel-injection system. Petrol has no lubricating element to it and the injectors do not need lubrication, so there is no need for a fuel return line. The fuel is supplied to the fuel rail and kept at a constant pressure ready for the fuel injectors to open. On older engines a carburettor replaces the fuel rail but the rest of the system is the same.

It is fairly common for petrol systems not to have a pre-filter and water separator, so the on-engine fuel filters are designed to separate water as well. Outboard engines often have an alarm that detects water in the fuel. Water in the fuel alarms are also sometimes fitted to inboard petrol and diesel engines. These can be identified by two electrical cables that will be attached to the bottom of the filter. Water will conduct electricity where fuel doesn't and will trigger the alarm.

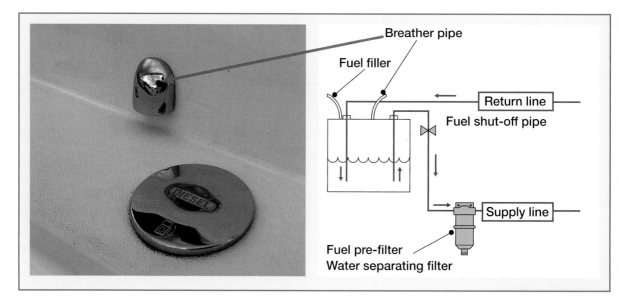

The fuel system diagram labels:
Breather pipe
Fuel filler
Return line
Fuel shut-off pipe
Supply line
Fuel pre-filter
Water separating filter

◆ The fuel tank

The fuel system starts with the fuel tank. Actually, it starts with the fuel filler on deck.

When you put fuel in the tank, the air inside needs to escape as the fuel enters and it vents through the fuel breather. If the fuel breather becomes blocked it is very difficult to fill the tank as the fuel gun will keep clicking off. The fuel breather on the outside of the boat, while covered, is open to the elements so check that it is clear.

One other thing about fuel on a boat is that water can enter the tank. There are five ways this can happen:

1. The most common cause is *through the filler cap*. When loose, perished or missing seals round the fuel filler cap let sea water and rainwater get into the tank.
2. *Cleaning the boat.* When cleaning and you squirt some water up the fuel breather, and this then goes into the tank.
3. *From condensation.* As the tank empties so the area of the tank, the walls that are exposed, increases and this is where droplets of water (condensation) will form. This water will encourage bacterial growth.
4. *Human error.* By someone – not usually the owner but someone trying to be helpful – mistaking the fuel tank for the water tank. It's more common than you might think!
5. *From fuel stations.* Fuel stations suffer from water build-up in their fuel tanks, exactly the same as you on your boat and if not noticed this fuel with added water will end up in your fuel tank.

▲ *Filling the fuel tank.*

Metal fuel tanks can rust internally and the rust can eventually block fuel lines and filters, leading to engine failure. It's worth having your fuel tank checked and cleaned just to make sure it is in tip-top condition.

◆ Fuel cut-off valve

Whenever you need to work on the engine fuel system or change filters you will need to shut off the fuel from the fuel tank so you need to locate the shut-off valve. It will be where the fuel pipe exits the fuel tank or close by for accessibility.

Sometimes there is no fuel shut-off valve, in which case the system is designed so that no fuel will leak out of the tank once you remove a filter, but obviously fuel in the line to that point and the fuel in the filter will need to be collected in a container, exactly as it would if you had a shut-off valve at the tank.

▲ *Fuel cut-off valves.*

◆ The pre-filter and water separator

The fuel feed pipe goes from the tank first to a pre-filter and water separator. This filter is not normally attached to the engine but is attached to a bulkhead. Sometimes you have to hunt around for them. There are also some systems where there is no pre-filter and water separator and the fuel line simply runs from the fuel tank directly to the on-engine fuel filter.

The pre-filter and water separator will be some distance from the engine so there is a gentle rise or drop from the fuel filter to the engine, to allow the fuel to flow smoothly and prevent air from becoming trapped at any high point.

In boats manufactured prior to the EU Recreational Craft Directive of June 1994 the fuel tank will often be higher than the engine, and in boats manufactured after this it will be lower than the engine where practical. The idea being that a tank below the engine reduces the chance of a spillage. Any high points in a fuel run should have a way of removing the air from the system, usually using a 'bleed screw' or 'bleed nipple'. Small amounts of air at these points may not affect fuel flow at low speeds because the fuel may flow under the

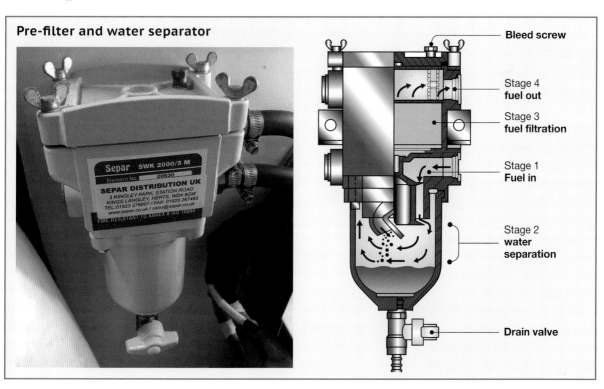

Pre-filter and water separator

Bleed screw

Stage 4
fuel out

Stage 3
fuel filtration

Stage 1
Fuel in

Stage 2
water separation

Drain valve

bubble but when the revs increase and more fuel is required then the air bubble will be pushed along the line and end up at the fuel injectors, causing the engine to lose power or cut out.

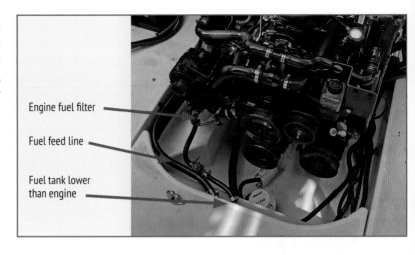

Engine fuel filter

Fuel feed line

Fuel tank lower than engine

◆ Fuel filters

From the pre-filter and the water separator the fuel feed pipe travels to the engine and will either:

1. attach to a low-pressure mechanical 'fuel lift pump', which pumps the fuel from the fuel tank then pushes it along a hose to the engine fuel filter, now under pressure;

2. attach to an electric fuel pump, which takes the place of the mechanical fuel lift pump;

3. attach straight on to the engine fuel filter. This is the case for ECU-controlled diesel engines where a high-pressure pump is used to inject the fuel into the cylinder.

The engine fuel filter is your 'last line of defence' against any contaminants in the fuel system.

Beyond this, on diesel engines, comes the high-pressure fuel pump, which distributes the fuel into metal fuel lines then on to the fuel injectors. This will provide the injector with pressurised fuel at the moment it requires it, to be injected into the cylinder when the air is fully compressed. Because of this, the pump is turned by the engine in time with the pistons and valves. It will either be geared to the crankshaft, have a timing chain or cambelt, or be directly operated via the camshaft.

The high-pressure fuel pump:
- supplies the correct amount of fuel to the injectors at high pressure (approx 200 bar)
- ensures the fuel is delivered to the injector at the top of the compression stroke

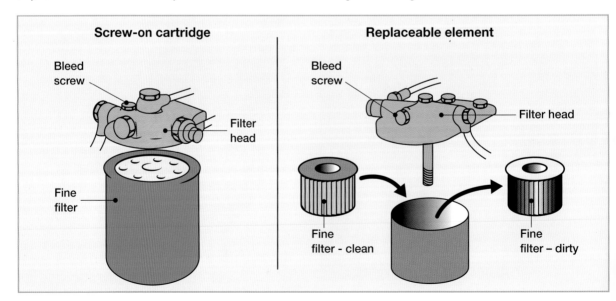

On-engine fuel filter and element

Filter cartridge

The new element ready

A bucket to catch any fuel as we remove the housing

Clean out the cartidge housing

In with the new element and back on with the filter. Check for leaks

◀ *Screw-on cartridge and replaceable element.*

- is extremely vulnerable to dirt and water internally
- is generally not user maintainable.

Or you could have a common rail system, where the pressure can reach over 2,000 bar as opposed to the 200 bar of the conventional diesel system.

A diesel common rail fuel system:
- uses an ECU to inject fuel, adjust the amount of fuel and the timing
- has a constant high-pressure pump, not timed like on a conventional diesel system
- uses a 'common rail' to store the high pressure ready for injection through the electronic fuel injectors controlled by the ECU.

The diesel common rail system is very similar to a petrol fuel injection system.

Next on a diesel engine come the injectors.

An injector:
- is a precision unit designed to deliver fuel at the correct pressure and spray pattern to the cylinder
- opens under fuel pressure produced by the injection pump
- ensures even and complete burning of the fuel
- is extremely vulnerable to dirt and water internally.

Next on a petrol engine comes the carburettor for mixing the fuel with air or a second higher-pressure fuel pump, which will fill a fuel rail ready for the electronic fuel injectors to use when required. The fuel injectors will be opened by an electric solenoid controlled by the ECU.

Carburettors are complicated, susceptible to dirt ingress and have many moving parts.

DIESEL BUG

Diesel bug is a term for various microbes that can find their way into your fuel tank and form a 'slug'-like jelly substance. Diesel bug needs water to promote its growth. It is generally a result of not turning over the fuel in the tank frequently enough, and if it gets into the fuel system can block a fuel line well before it ever reaches a filter.

There are additives for diesel bug with which you can treat the fuel to prevent bacteria from growing. Diesel bug is particularly fond of bio-diesel and as bio-diesel becomes the standard

for cars and boats, so the use of anti-diesel-bug additives will become more and more important.

But prevention being better than cure, you can help yourself by:

1. turning over the fuel in the tank frequently
2. keeping the tank full to prevent the build-up of condensation on the sides of the tank
3. ensuring that the fuel filler cap is properly sealed and does not allow any water into the tank.

Points 2 and 3 we have said already but they really are very important.

Changing filters

Filters need to be changed at the regular service interval, which is usually every year or after 100 engine hours.

◆ Pre-filter and water separator

1. Turn off the fuel by the tank, if it has a shut-off valve.
2. With a bowl ready to collect the diesel and water, unscrew the drain outlet on the bottom of the clear bowl or closed bowl, depending on the type of water separator.
3. Loosen the bleed screw on top of the pre-filter to allow air to enter the top of the filter, helping the fuel to run out of the drain.
4. Unscrew or dismantle the pre-filter to remove the fuel filter element and replace. Reassemble the filter using new seals and fill with fuel if possible. If it cannot be filled, don't worry as we can bleed it at the engine end later.

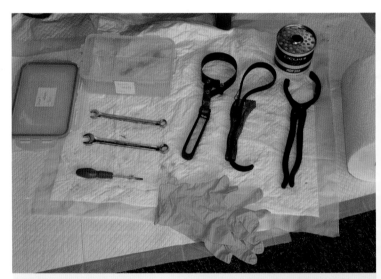

▲ *Tools for the job – including grips of varying strength to remove the filter, sealable receptacles for the diesel and the new filter.*

Bleed screw

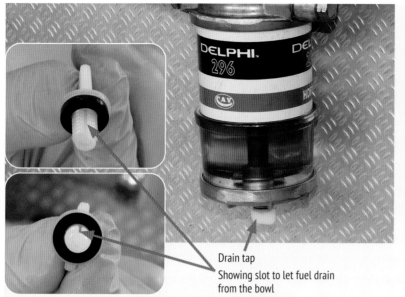

Drain tap
Showing slot to let fuel drain
from the bowl

▲ Bowl removed.

▲ Removing the old filter.

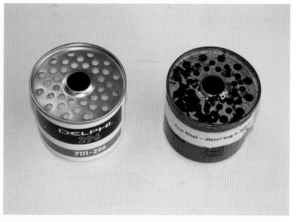

▲ The new and the old.

▲ The new filter.

▲ Job done and filling with diesel.

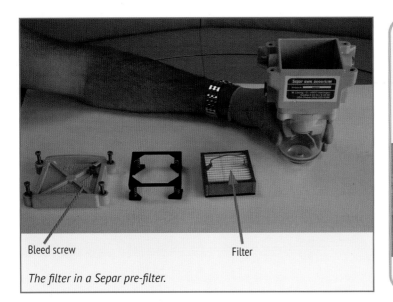

Bleed screw   Filter

The filter in a Separ pre-filter.

TIP

Make sure you have a sealable container to put waste fuel and fuel filters in. It is easy to knock over an open container in an enclosed space.

Full of diesel.

◆ On-engine fuel filters

These are normally just a screw-on canister. Sometimes they can have a removable element but neither type collects water, unless there is a drain screw on the bottom. Usually, these filters just filter the fuel and do not separate water, which is why you need a pre-filter.

1. With the fuel shut off at the tank shut-off valve, if there is one, and a bowl ready to catch any spillage, unscrew the fuel filter, which will be full of fuel.
2. If it has a replaceable element, replace this with a new element and screw the filter back in place.
3. Or, if it is the type where you replace the entire filter, then simply replace the filter with a new one.
4. Remember to dispose of the element/old filter in the correct bin in the boatyard.
5. Do not fill the engine fuel filter with fuel before screwing it back on, unless told to do so by the engine manufacturer, as you do not want to introduce unfiltered fuel to the downstream side of the fuel system.
6. Turn the fuel back on.
7. Before bleeding the air from the fuel pre-filter and the on-engine fuel filter, loosen the bleed screw on the on-engine fuel filter, if one is fitted. If a bleed screw is not fitted, this will mean bleeding is not required and so the engine should start after a few tries (this applies to most petrol engines).
8. Pump the mechanical lift pump using the lever or plunger fitted to it.

9. Or, turn on the ignition to run the electric fuel pump.
10. Or, if there is no lift pump use the hand pump, which is usually fitted to the top of the engine fuel filter, or the in-line hand bulb type pump.
11. In any case, pump until fuel with no bubbles comes out of the bleed screw, then stop and tighten the bleed screw back up, being careful not to overtighten as they can fracture easily.
12. If there is no bleed screw fitted – which applies to most petrol outboard engines – operate the hand pump until it becomes firm.
13. Start the engine. If it does not start or starts and cuts out, repeat from step 6.

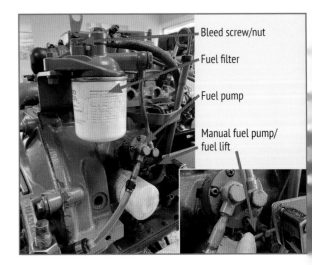

Bleed screw/nut

Fuel filter

Fuel pump

Manual fuel pump/ fuel lift

Light

Medium

Heavy

▲ *Fuel filter grips.*

▲ *Remove the old filter and fit the new.*

Bleed screw

▲ *Some paper towel around the filter will catch the fuel as it comes out of the bleed screw.*

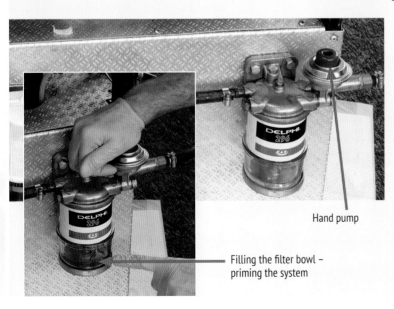

Hand pump

Filling the filter bowl – priming the system

Scan this QR code to watch a video on bleeding an engine.

Scan this QR code to watch a video on changing a primary fuel/water separator filter.

Scan this QR code to watch a video on changing an on-engine fuel filter.

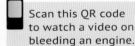

Symptoms of fuel-system breakdowns

Here are the most common symptoms of breakdowns in fuel systems and what we can do about them.

◆ Blockage in the fuel system

Signs: The engine will lose power and cut out.

Engines always start regardless of whether there is a blockage in the fuel system or not because there is always some residual fuel in the engine. You can even start a diesel engine with the fuel off. It will run for a short time on the residual fuel in the system, then reduce revs and cut out.

So, assuming that the fuel is on and there is fuel in the tank, if the engine starts and then reduces revs and cuts out there is a blockage and fuel cannot reach the cylinder.

Causes?

- There could be a fuel system blockage. This will be somewhere between the fuel tank and the first fuel filter in the system, which may be a pre-filter and water separator or the on-engine filter.
- The filter element may be so contaminated it will no longer allow fuel to flow through it so check this first.
- There could be a blockage in the fuel standpipe (the pipe that runs from the top of the tank to the bottom of the tank to suck up the fuel). Most fuel standpipes have a gauze over the end and this can clog up.
- If no gauze is fitted, the blockage will be found where the pipe first narrows. In other words, where the fuel pipe goes into a hose tail. This could be by the fuel shut-off valve or where the hose fits to the pre-filter.

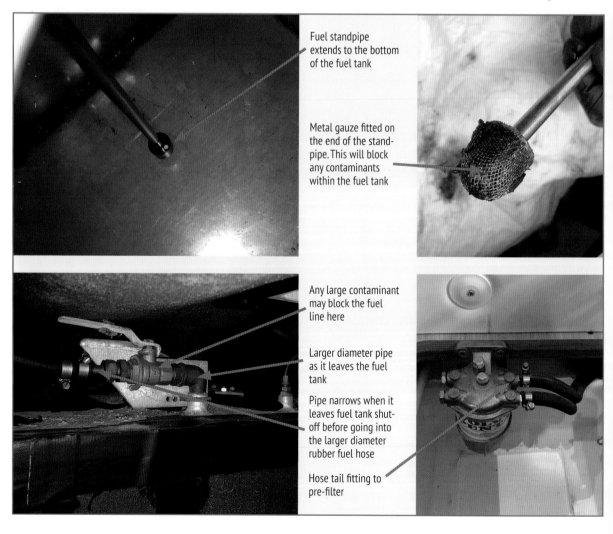

Fuel standpipe extends to the bottom of the fuel tank

Metal gauze fitted on the end of the stand-pipe. This will block any contaminants within the fuel tank

Any large contaminant may block the fuel line here

Larger diameter pipe as it leaves the fuel tank

Pipe narrows when it leaves fuel tank shut-off before going into the larger diameter rubber fuel hose

Hose tail fitting to pre-filter

1. Insert a pipe (1) for the siphon into the can. Make sure it goes to the bottom of the can and then insert the other end into the tank filler pipe,
2. Make sure the bottom of the fuel can is higher than the end of the pipe being lowered into the tank for the siphon to work.
3. Take another piece of pipe (2) and insert into the can. Leave the end of this pipe at the top of the can.
4. Wrap a cloth round the top of the can to make a seal around the two pipes and the mouth of the can.
5. Blow into pipe (2). This will build pressure in the can sufficient to get the fuel up the siphon pipe (1) and flowing into the tank.
6. When the fuel starts to flow you can stop blowing and remove the cloth and pipe (2). The siphon will suck the fuel from the can into the tank.

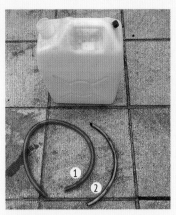

▲ *The kit, 1 × can, 2 × pipes, thick (1) and thin (2).*

▲ *Insert the thick pipe below the liquid and the thin pipe above the liquid. Cover the opening as best you can to stop air escaping and blow.*

Watch this video to see how to siphon from a can into a tank without getting a mouthful of fuel.

◆ Mechanical fuel system problems

Signs: On a diesel engine, if the starter motor is able to turn the engine over but the engine doesn't catch, not even a cough or a splutter, and the engine stops turning over when the starter motor stops, the problem is likely to be a mechanical one.

On a petrol engine, this symptom indicates a mechanical problem, probably spark ignition or fuel pump related.

Causes?
- A problem with the fuel pump(s).
- Fuel 'stop handle' in the stop position, 'kill cord' not inserted, or the 'run-stop' switch in the incorrect position.
- Internal engine failure is causing the stroke cycle to stop operating. This could be as a result of a broken crankshaft.
- Failure of the spark ignition system on a petrol engine.
- A fuse might have blown or tripped out, somewhere in the electrical system.

DIESEL TIP

If you have a non-ECU-controlled diesel engine, loosen the fuel pipes that are attached directly to the fuel injectors, turn the engine over and observe:

- If no fuel comes out at all you have a fuel problem.
- If fuel squirts out, it is likely to be an internal mechanical problem.
- Before stripping the engine down, do check what it is that is coming out. It could be water, which would be a result of water in the fuel. It could be petrol because someone has filled up with the wrong fuel.

Remember a diesel engine only requires fuel and air to run.

◆ Air in the system

Signs: If an engine starts up and then cuts out straight away, it suggests that there is unwanted air in the system. Air in the fuel line can happen if the fuel tank is below the level of the engine. As fuel is heavier than air, gravity will pull the fuel back towards the fuel tank, leaving air above it. Finding the point at which air is entering the fuel system can be quite challenging.

Causes?

Common causes of air ingress are:

* out of fuel!!
* badly fitted or perished fuel filter seals
* bleed screw washers damaged or loose
* hose fittings loose
* chaffed or split fuel lines.

Showing direction of flow arrow

▲ *This fuel priming bulb is the same as one used on an outboard engine to prime it.*

The best way to find out where air is entering the system is:

1. Turn off the fuel at the fuel tank.
2. Remove the pipe from the fuel lift pump or on-engine fuel filter if no pump is fitted.
3. Fit a small in-line fuel priming bulb – these are available at your local chandler – to the detached hose so the direction of flow goes back towards the

▲ *1. Turn off the fuel at the tank.*

▲ *2. The tools for the job.*

▲ *3. Remove the fuel pipe from the fuel pump.*

▲ *4. You're now ready for the fuel priming bulb.*

▲ 5. Fit the fuel priming bulb with the arrow facing down the fuel pipe that you want to pressurise.

▲ 6. Give it several pumps until it is hard to get pressure in the system.

fuel tank. As long as you fit the priming bulb so that the arrow on it is pointing towards the fuel tank, all will be well.

4. Pump the bulb and this will pressurise the fuel line from the engine end all the way through the water separator and to the fuel tank.

5. Now any loose fittings or damaged seals will have air or fuel leaking from them – easy!!

6. Repair the problem and then refit the hose and bleed the engine.

▶ 7. You can see air bubbles in the bowl of the pre-filter when you squeeze. At this point, fuel should be seeping out of wherever there is an air leak into the fuel system.

Fuel tanks and gauges

It's a good idea to keep the fuel tank as full as possible and certainly above half full for a number of reasons:

- It reduces the risk of moisture forming on the tank walls and getting water in the fuel.
- Fuel gauges are notoriously inaccurate and often a gauge showing half full actually has a good deal less than half in the tank.
- Very low fuel in the tank will stir up sediment at the bottom of the tank, leading to blocked filters.
- Very low fuel combined with heeling could lead to the fuel pick-up line becoming momentarily uncovered, which would create an air bubble in the fuel line, starve the engine of fuel and cause it to cut out.

Always make sure you have plenty of fuel before setting off on any passage.

◆ Fuel gauge senders

There are two types of sender:

1. A linear sender where a metal arm with a float drops down in the tank as the fuel level reduces and as the float drops so the electronic resistance increases. This provides a reasonably regular sweep and gives a fairly reliable reading.

2. A plastic float that goes up and down a metal rod with different resistances at different levels. But these resistances are in sections and so a change in reading only occurs when the plastic float moves from one

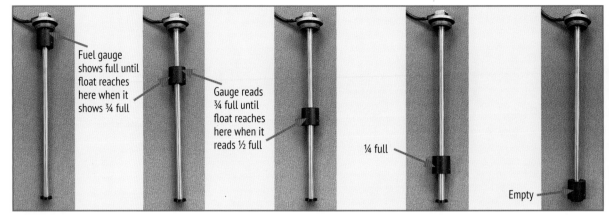

Fuel gauge shows full until float reaches here when it shows ¾ full

Gauge reads ¾ full until float reaches here when it reads ½ full

¼ full

Empty

▲ *Here is an example of a non-linear/non-graduated sender – the Wema.*

section or level of resistance to the next and you do not get a smooth sweep of a reading. Unfortunately, these are becoming more common due to the fact that they are more robust than the linear type, which have a number of exposed electrical connections that are subject to corrosion.

The plastic float senders that do not give a linear reading might be calibrated to show eighths of a tank or, worse, quarters of a tank. Here, the gauge might be showing half full when you set off, which might be enough fuel for your trip. What you wouldn't know is if the amount of fuel was very nearly at the quarter-full mark, which the gauge would not show until it reached this level. You could end up leaving the berth thinking you had half a tank and within a couple of minutes find you actually only had a quarter of a tank.

◆ Monitoring fuel consumption

It is essential to monitor fuel consumption and record it. Always fill the tank(s) to the brim. Note the engine hours at each fill-up and the litres or gallons of fuel – it will be on the fuel receipt usually. Then work out your average hourly fuel consumption, bearing in mind the sort of motoring you were doing. Keep a note of this for every fill-up to get an average of your fuel consumption at each fill-up.

Then you can monitor the fuel gauge by looking at the engine hours since the last fill-up and multiplying these by the average hourly consumption to know what has been used. Take this away from the tank capacity to estimate what you have left.

◆ Fuel dipstick

Dipping a stick into the tank and seeing how far up the stick shows as wet does not tell you how much fuel is in the tank, simply that there is fuel in the tank. Quite often, fuel tanks are shaped to fit the hull especially in sailing boats.

You might have a 'V'-shaped tank and the stick might show 10 inches worth of fuel but this is going to represent very little as against 10 inches in a rectangular tank.

If you want the dipstick to be meaningful, you need to graduate it. This is not something for larger boats as it is something of a faff and fairly impractical.

Say your engine uses 3 litres per hour, a safe margin before running out might be 10 litres of fuel – 3 hours of running. With the tank empty you pour 10 litres of fuel into the tank. Mark where this comes to on your stick. Then add 25 litres and mark this, and then 50 litres and another 50 litres etc. Now your stick is calibrated in 50-litre intervals with a 35-litre warning level and then the 10-litre nearly empty level. As I said, it is a faff but it is more accurate than any fuel gauge.

◆ Polishing fuel

This is the process of passing fuel through water separators and fuel filters to remove any water, debris and diesel bug. This would usually be done in conjunction with cleaning the fuel tank. You would remove the fuel from the tank, polish it and store it, clean the tank and then put the polished fuel back into the tank and add an anti-diesel-bug treatment to it when you do so.

▲ *The Wema readout.*

▶ *If the fuel gauge is measuring depth of fuel, then the readings between the tanks will differ greatly.*

Fuel gauge – what is it telling us?

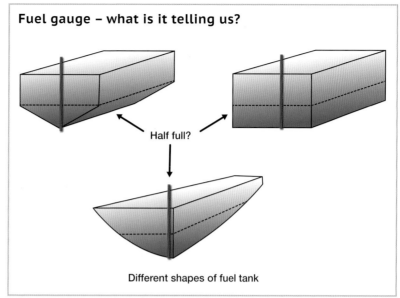

Different shapes of fuel tank

You would then treat the fuel with an anti-diesel-bug additive at each fill-up and aim to keep the fuel tank as full as possible at all times to avoid condensation build-up and keep bacterial growth at bay.

To prevent bacterial growth from getting to a stage where it becomes a problem, it is advisable to clean your fuel tank every five years

◆ The wrong fuel!

What happens if you don't know the difference between a diesel and petrol engine and you put the wrong fuel into the tank?

Well, it will stop running, for a start.

It is worth considering the differences between the two fuels.

Diesel is essentially a very refined oil. So apart from being a fuel it is also a lubricant. Diesel is very inert – there are no vapours that come off it. If you leave it in an open container, it doesn't evaporate and it is not very combustible. You could throw a match into it and it probably wouldn't ignite – don't try this, for obvious reasons.

Petrol, which is taken off higher up the fractionating process of crude oil is very volatile. It fumes, it will evaporate if left in the open and it is highly flammable.

Dipping the fuel tank – what does it tell us?

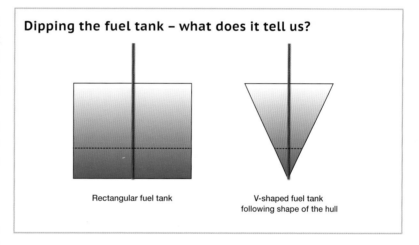

Rectangular fuel tank

V-shaped fuel tank following shape of the hull

◆ Diesel in a petrol engine

If you have put diesel into a petrol engine you will find that the spark from the spark plug will not be sufficient to ignite the diesel, added to which the oil within the diesel will coat the spark plug and prevent it from sparking.

You will need to:

1. Empty the fuel tank.
2. Take out and clean the spark plugs.
3. Make sure the fuel system is clean of diesel.
4. Change the fuel filters including any pre-filter and water separator.

Then fill her up with petrol and she should start.

◆ Petrol in a diesel engine

You do not want to do this because it can damage the engine.

Again, the engine will stop because although there is no spark in a diesel engine, petrol being a lighter fuel than diesel will ignite under compression but it will do so much sooner than diesel – under much less compression. And so, the petrol will ignite about halfway through the compression cycle, which is too early in the sequence and this will send the piston down too early. This igniting too early in the sequence is called 'pre-ignition' and the result is that the engine will bang and stop.

Also, there is no lubrication element to petrol and the elements within a diesel engine use the oil within the diesel fuel for lubrication. So you can end up with damage to the fuel injectors and the high-pressure fuel pump.

You will need to:

1. Empty the fuel tank.
2. Make sure the fuel system is clean of petrol.
3. Change the fuel filters including the pre-filter and water separator.

Then fill her up with diesel...

But before you try to start her, you will need to prime the engine. You see, running out of diesel means that you now have air in the system. And while a petrol engine can purge air out of the system if it runs out of fuel, a standard diesel engine with a lift pump that is driven off the engine cannot. Some diesel engines have electric fuel pumps and there is no need to bleed the system. But for those without you will need to bleed the system. To do this:

1. Find the fuel primer pump or lift pump. This could be a push button, a large bulb or a small lever.
2. Loosen the bleed screw a couple of turns. This allows air to 'bleed' out of the fuel line as air is pulled from the tank to the fuel filter.
3. Pump the primer or manual lever for the lift pump until diesel comes out of the bleed screw.
4. Tighten the bleed screw.
5. Start the engine.
6. If the engine does not start within 15 seconds or so there may still be air in the fuel line and you will need to repeat the bleed process.

▲ *Manual fuel lift pumps*

▲ *Bleed screws*

Jonathan says

A family picked up a RIB they had hired, took it off the dock and it broke down a few hundred yards up the river, narrowly avoiding an accident and they had to tie up alongside another vessel moored in the river. I then received a call-out to rescue them. I tried to start the engine. It turned over without starting but coughed a few times and I was about to take the outboard engine cover off when I got a call from the owner...

But before we find out about that call, I discovered later that the RIB had been hired out the day before and the charterers were new to the boat and generally inexperienced. In fact, it was the first time they had hired a boat from anyone. They had a great day out on the water and were charged with filling the boat back up with fuel on their return. Fortunately, there is a fuel berth about 300 yards from where the boat is kept so they pulled up to refuel. The fuel bay was attended at this time and a fuel pump was handed over and was taken by them without question – well, why would they, as inexperienced boaters, question an attendant whom they assumed knew what they were doing as it was their job? The engine started fine and they got back the 300 yards to the berth with no problem.

Now back to the phone call. The owner had just looked at the fuel receipt from the customers who had hired the RIB the day before. They had returned the RIB full of fuel – only the receipt said diesel and not petrol!!

There had been sufficient petrol in the system to get the inexperienced boaters back to the charter office the day before, so they were none the wiser.

Now armed with this news, I towed the RIB back to the charter office. We had to lift the boat out of the water as we needed to remove some engine components. We drained the tank of 150 litres, flushed the fuel system through, changed the fuel filters and then filled back up with petrol.

This was a costly exercise and came about as a result of an assumption and inexperience. It was later discovered that the fuel attendant was new and as she was busy hadn't realised that the boat was petrol. Handing the pump over, she assumed she would be told by the 'owner' of the RIB if she was giving them the wrong fuel. The inexperienced charterer, assuming of course that the attendant would know which pump to hand over, took it without question. An easy mistake to make maybe, but because neither the attendant nor the charterer checked, not only was it an expensive mistake but it put others in danger – the family I was attending to. It will have ruined their day out boating and it will also have knocked their confidence.

Moral of the story – NEVER ASSUME!

5 Cooling systems

There are two types of cooling system on the marine engine.

Raw-water system

The body of water you are floating in, be it sea or fresh water, is pumped around the outside of the internal parts of the engine in what are called cooling galleries by a raw-water pump, also called an impeller pump. There needs to be a constant flow of water around the system not just to keep the engine at its operating temperature but also to lubricate and cool the working parts such as the rubber impeller and exhaust system. Raw water goes to the pump and then splits, one feed going to the cooling galleries and the other to the exhaust. Once the water exits the cooling galleries, it will join the feed to the exhaust and both are pumped out of the boat via the exhaust pipe outlet.

There is a thermostat on the engine side to keep the raw water in the cooling galleries at a constant temperature round the engine. When it closes, all the raw water will circulate within the cooling galleries until it reopens, enabling cooler water to enter. This process can repeat quickly or slowly depending on engine load and speed but the end goal is for the temperature to stay as constant as possible within the engine. We will explain this further, later in the chapter.

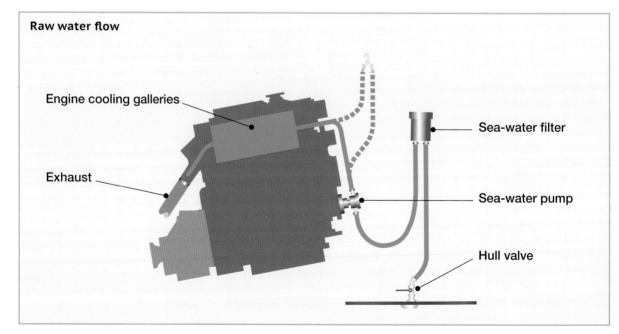

Raw water flow

Engine cooling galleries

Exhaust

Sea-water filter

Sea-water pump

Hull valve

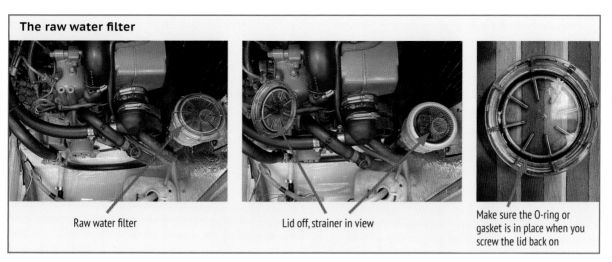

Raw water filter

Lid off, strainer in view

Make sure the O-ring or gasket is in place when you screw the lid back on

▲ *Raw-water filter with strainer. Daily engine checks should ensure that this is free from obstruction. When removing the lid, do be aware of the O-ring/gasket in the lid and make sure this is in place when you put the lid back, otherwise you will create an air gap and very quickly you will find that your engine is overheating as the raw water will not flow through the system.*

Fresh-water and raw-water system

Here, instead of cooling the engine directly, the raw water for cooling the engine is fed to a heat exchanger. The heat exchanger contains a series of pipes – a heat exchanger bundle – through which the raw water flows. The heat exchanger bundle is then housed within a casing, through which the fresh water and antifreeze mix (coolant) flows. This coolant circulates round the outside of the internal parts of the engine in the cooling galleries and is cooled by the raw water flowing through the bundle of pipes in the heat exchanger. The coolant is pumped round this 'closed' system by a circulation pump, driven usually by the drive belt.

There is a header tank for topping up the coolant, with maximum and minimum level marks to ensure the system is kept full.

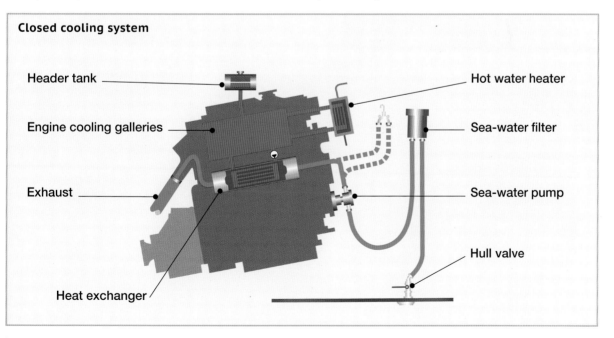

Closed cooling system

Header tank

Engine cooling galleries

Exhaust

Heat exchanger

Hot water heater

Sea-water filter

Sea-water pump

Hull valve

The coolant will reach close to boiling point in the closed system. It will expand and if this expansion becomes excessive due to the engine overheating, the pressure build-up will be released through the header tank cap.

There is no thermostat on the raw-water side of this system but there is a thermostat on the closed side of the system to ensure that the engine is kept at a constant temperature.

In a boat, cool raw water takes the place of cool air in a car. A car engine is cooled by coolant in a closed system, which cools the engine's internal parts. This coolant is then cooled by the radiator, which radiates

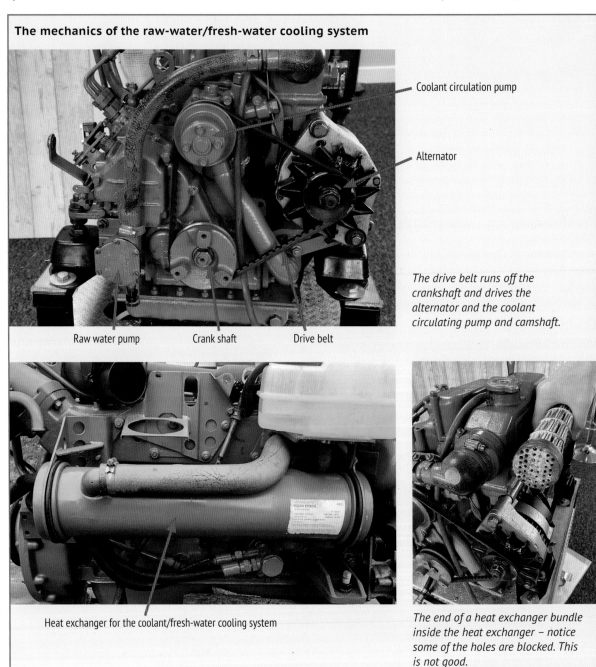

The mechanics of the raw-water/fresh-water cooling system

Coolant circulation pump

Alternator

The drive belt runs off the crankshaft and drives the alternator and the coolant circulating pump and camshaft.

Raw water pump   Crank shaft   Drive belt

Heat exchanger for the coolant/fresh-water cooling system

The end of a heat exchanger bundle inside the heat exchanger – notice some of the holes are blocked. This is not good.

this heat into the air stream as the car moves. There is no opportunity for this on a boat as the engine is in an enclosed space and so raw water is used to cool the heat exchanger as the hot coolant passes through it, just as air does in a car's radiator. There may be a number of heat exchangers fitted to your engine and we will talk about these later in the chapter.

Common causes of overheating

Any of the following could warn you that the engine is overheating:

- Engine temperature alarm going off
- Engine temperature gauge higher than normal
- Excess steam from the exhaust outlet
- No water from the exhaust outlet
- Engine radiates excessive heat (feels and smells hotter than normal)

The engine will stop if it gets so hot that the metal in the engine expands to the point that the internal moving parts seize up.

◆ Raw-water inlet blockage

Weed, fish, barnacles, plastic bags blocking the raw-water inlet.

What to do?

If your raw-water strainer is above the waterline of the boat:

1. Take a dinghy foot pump.
2. Take the lid off the raw-water strainer, remove the basket and check that this is clear of debris.
3. Poke the hose of the pump down inside the body of the raw-water strainer until it is in the hose for the raw-water inlet.
4. Place a cloth over the top of the raw-water strainer (to help provide a seal in the event that the pump hose is not a tight fit in the raw-water pipe) and start pumping.

The minute you hear bubbles blowing out under the hull, you have cleared the blockage. Always pump another 10 times to make sure that the inlet is clear. Then replace the strainer, and the lid to the raw-water strainer ensuring that the O-ring seal is in place, and start the engine. Raise the engine speed to get the water pumping well. Initially, the impeller will be having to pump air through the system until it sucks up the raw water. One way round this is to prime the raw-water strainer. So before replacing the lid to the raw-water strainer, do the following:

1. Close the sea cock.
2. Fill the raw-water strainer to the top with water.
3. Replace the lid, checking that the O-ring seal is in place – now the system is sealed and the water you added to the strainer will not drain away as it would have if you had left the sea cock open – the raw-water filter being above the water level.
4. Open sea cock – and start the engine.

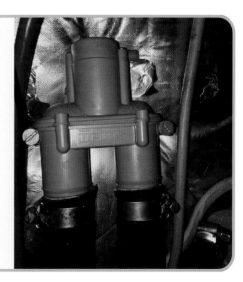

SIPHON BREAKS / VENTED LOOPS

These are used anywhere on a boat to prevent water, usually raw water, siphoning into the system when the engine is not running. For example, if a raw-water pump has a worn impeller that does not provide a good seal, raw water can pass through the system, fill up the exhaust, back up into the exhaust manifold and into a cylinder via an open exhaust valve – water in the engine.

Siphon breaks can be either a simple air gap or a valve. All siphon breaks need to be checked annually to ensure they are not blocked. The valve type, which open only when a certain pressure is reached, are subject to blocking. Replace the valve with a new one of the correct pressure rating.

If your raw-water strainer is below the waterline of the boat:

1. Take a dinghy foot pump.
2. Shut off the raw-water sea cock – to prevent water flooding into the boat.
3. Take the lid off the raw-water strainer, remove the basket and check that this is clear of debris.
4. Poke the hose of the pump down inside the body of the raw-water strainer until it is in the hose for the raw-water inlet.
5. Place a cloth over the top of the raw-water strainer (to help provide a seal in the event that the pump hose is not a tight fit in the raw-water pipe) and start pumping. This will build up pressure to help dislodge the blockage.
6. Open the raw-water sea cock.
7. When you hear bubbles, pump 10 more times to ensure the inlet is clear.
8. Close the sea cock.

After closing the sea cock, replace the strainer and the lid to the raw-water strainer, ensuring that the O-ring seal is in place. Open the sea cock then start the engine and raise the engine speed to get the water pumping well.

HOW TO CHANGE A DRIVE BELT

Loosen here ...

... and here

Loosen the bolt at the top and the bolt on the adjustable plate. Swing the alternator to the left in this case to release tension and remove the old belt. Fit the new one. Swing the alternator to the right and tension until there is about 1cm (1.4 – ½ inch) of play in total and tighten the two bolts.

▲ *Dinghy pump hose down raw-water inlet pipe.*

◆ **Drive belt broken**

... or too slack and not turning the water pump? If the belt is broken, this should be fairly obvious.

What to do?

First, check to see why the drive belt might have broken.
- Are the pulleys seized?
- Are the pulleys loose as a result of bearing failure?
- Are they out of line with the other pulleys?
- Are any of the bolts or nuts on the components to which the pulleys attach loose?

If the answer is no, the drive belt may have broken because it was worn out. In this case, simply replace the belt. The engine operator's manual will advise you how to fit a new belt and how to adjust the belt tension.

Never over-tighten the belt as it will overload the bearings of the driven components, leading to premature failure.

If you are unsure of the belt tension, a simple rule is to press down on it midway between 2 pulleys and you should not be able to move it more than 0.5cm (¼ inch).

Another tip for establishing the correct drive belt tension is to turn the alternator pulley by its cooling fins. If the pulley and belt turn together, the tension is OK. If the pulley turns but the belt does not then it is 'slipping' and needs to be tightened up.

Belts attached and running	Belts removed

Raw water pump   Coolant circulation pump   Crankshaft pulley   Alternator

▲ *Alternator belt and pulleys.*

Cooling fins

▲ *Without the engine running, try to turn the alternator pulley using the cooling fins. If it turns and the belt does not, tighten the belt.*

◆ **Broken impeller**

For this you will need to unscrew the impeller plate and have a look at the impeller.

What to do?

1. Check that the raw-water sea cock is closed.
2. Remove pump/impeller cover screws and cover.
3. If fitted (rare,) remove any impeller locking device.
4. Remove cover seal/gasket.

5. Using an impeller puller/polygrip/pliers, remove the impeller.
6. Where the impeller cover meets the housing, clean both the surface of the impeller cover and the surrounding where it connects to the impeller pump housing to remove any corrosion or deposits.
   Tip: A small scraper, WD-40 and a green scouring pad work best.
7. Fit the new impeller, covering with glycerine gel or washing-up liquid. This is to ensure that the impeller is lubricated when we come to start the engine for the first time with the new impeller. Ensure the blades are bent in the correct direction for pump rotation.
   Tip: Take a photo of the old impeller before you remove it to remind you of which way the blades were bent.
8. Fit the new cover seal/gasket using a small amount of waterproof grease to help hold it in place.
9. Replace pump/impeller cover and cover screws.
10. Open raw-water sea cock before starting engine.
11. Most important of all, check to see that water is coming out of the exhaust. This tells you that raw water is running round the system. If you used washing-up liquid on the impeller, you will see bubbles coming out of the exhaust system too.

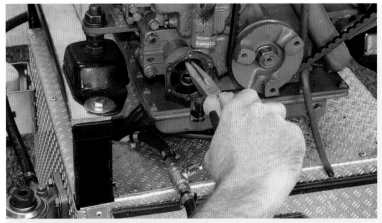

▲ *Pliers removing an impeller.*

▲ *Sometimes you need an impeller puller like this...*

▼ *...especially if the impeller is large.*

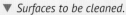

▼ *Surfaces to be cleaned.*

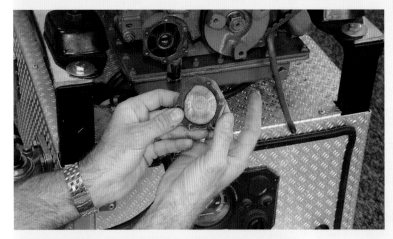

Scan this QR code to watch a video showing you how to change an impeller.

▲ *A Speedseal cover – no longer made but if you have one of these then removing and replacing the cover is much quicker than standard nuts. (courtesy of Sea Start)*

▲ *Water coming out of the exhaust of an inboard diesel.*

▲ *If it looks like this then you need to replace it.*   ▲ *This is what it should look like.*

If the impeller is missing any of its blades, they might have gone further along the cooling system, but if the impeller has failed because of a lack of raw water then the blades will be subject to gravity and will have fallen down the system into either the inlet or outlet pipe – and we need to find them.

If your impeller housing, water strainer and the hoses to it are below the waterline, take the inlet pipe off the impeller housing and have a container at the ready to catch any water. Open the sea cock to flush any blades out of this section of the pipe.

If your raw-water strainer is above the waterline, simply turn off the sea cock, remove the lid of the strainer, take off the pipe to the impeller housing and pour water into the strainer to flush the pipe.

If nothing comes out, close the sea cock and reattach the inlet pipe to the impeller housing. Now take the outlet pipe off the impeller housing and off the heat exchanger end and blow through it to clean it. If nothing is found here, then the blades may be in the heat exchanger and you can look in there with a torch and using a hooked tool remove the blades. If this is unsuccessful – and by now we are getting pretty involved with the engine – you need to remove the end of the heat exchanger and it is probably time to call an engineer!

Nine times out of ten, overheating will be an issue with the raw-water inlet or the strainer.

Two pieces of kit worth having are an infrared thermometer, especially if you have a twin-engine boat and you want to see which engine is the hotter of the two, and an endoscope to look down pipes, into heat exchangers and so forth to find loose blades and debris. Endoscopes come with a hook, a light and a magnet to help you remove bits.

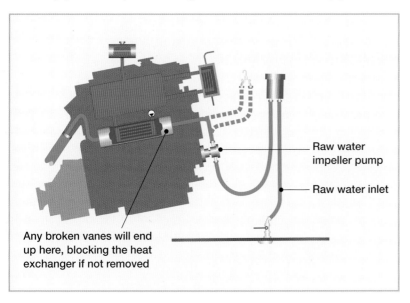

Raw water impeller pump

Raw water inlet

Any broken vanes will end up here, blocking the heat exchanger if not removed

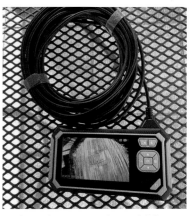

▲ *An endoscope can be useful for checking that pipes are clear of obstructions and they come with a selection of tools to help you remove debris.*

HEAT EXCHANGERS

You can have more than one heat exchanger on a boat. The engine on a yacht will probably just have one heat exchanger to cool the coolant in the closed system with the raw water passing through the heat exchanger. But there are also heat exchangers for cooling the engine oil, gearbox oil, power-steering oil and for cooling the turbo air, which, as it pumps air at high pressure back into the cylinder air inlet, creates a great deal of heat. There are even heat exchangers for cooling the fuel, generally to be found on some high-performance engines to prevent the fuel from getting too hot in the system.

IS A HEAT EXCHANGER WORKING PROPERLY?

Measure the temperature where the pipe for what is being cooled enters the heat exchanger then measure the temperature of the pipe after it has exited the heat exchanger. There should be a temperature difference. A drop of about 6°C for coolant and gearbox oil is about right and a drop of between 6°C and 12°C for oil that is being cooled is to be expected. If the differences are less, then the heat exchanger is blocked, or the pipes in the bundle have furred up.

Infrared thermometer (or pyrometer) showing radiator 45.6°C showing laser pointer.

◆ Failure of the raw-water and fresh-water system thermostats

Both the raw-water only and raw-water/coolant systems have thermostats, which are designed to trap the water in the engine until it reaches the correct operating temperature, then regulate the flow of water to keep it at a constant temperature. A thermostat is basically a valve that opens and shuts. It is usually maintenance-free but can suffer with corrosion on raw-water-only cooled engines – the raw water often being sea water. Closed system engines are protected from corrosion because the coolant is a mix of fresh water and antifreeze, which contains corrosion inhibitors.

If a thermostat fails, it won't release the water to cool the engine. The engine temperature will therefore keep increasing until either you notice that the temperature gauge is off the clock, the alarm goes off and you stop the engine, or the metal in the engine expands to the point that it seizes and stops.

On rare occasions, a thermostat can fail in the open position. This is more common on raw-water-only cooling systems as a result of corrosion. If the thermostat jams in the open position, the engine won't overheat but the engine temperature will vary greatly. Instead of balancing the temperature of the cooling water to that of the engine, you will find that raising the engine speed passes more cold water through the system, which cools the engine internals too quickly. When you increase

the revs, you have cold water entering a hot engine and this difference in temperatures can fatigue the metal in the engine. Reducing the engine revs means the water flow will slow and the engine temperature will increase but it will never get hotter than its normal running temperature. So, if you suspect the thermostat is stuck in the open position, reduce the engine speed. The point of the cooling system is to keep all the metal components within the engine at the correct temperature constantly, as all the internal components of the engine are designed to expand with temperature to certain tolerances. If you can't control that temperature, they can either over- or under-expand. If they over expand, they can seize up and if they under-expand they can experience excessive wear. So, it's really important that the cooling temperature remains constant in the engine. Because of the potential for corrosion of a thermostat in a raw-water system, the thermostat should be changed every three years. A thermostat in a raw-water/coolant system can last for the lifetime of the engine.

WHY ENGINE TEMPERATURE IS SO IMPORTANT

Engines have an optimum working temperature; anything less than this will wear them out more quickly, as will anything greater than this. The greatest amount of wear to an engine comes when they are warming up to operating temperature. The longer this takes, the greater the wear on the engine.

So, when you start your engine from cold, put it in gear on the dock and raise the engine speed to 1,000 to 1,200 revs. This will put it under load straight away, which will get it to warm up as quickly as possible and your engine will last you that much longer. The engine has to work harder when turning the propeller through the water, it introduces more fuel to increase the power, this then creates a bigger bang in the combustion chamber, which in turn creates more heat and so warms the engine quicker. Running the engine in neutral for 30 minutes heats the engine up very slowly and won't get it up to temperature in that time. A diesel engine needs to be under load to heat up quickly. So start the engine, run it for a minute and as soon as the engine has 'settled down', click it into gear and it will get up to temperature within the next 15 minutes or so.

Cooling system for an outboard engine

All outboards are raw-water cooled; they have an impeller, which requires removal of the gearbox to gain access to it. This can be undertaken by most DIY engineers but you will need instruction to do this, either from the engine manual or better still from an experienced engineer, to avoid damage or breaking components.

Exhaust systems

Engine exhaust temperatures can get to over 500°C and engine exhaust pipes are usually made of rubber, which is rated to 120°C. Much over this and it will start to weaken and then eventually melt. So the exhaust system needs to be cooled and this is done by the raw water, which has cooled the engine either directly or via a heat exchanger in a closed system – the raw water exiting the boat via the exhaust, along with the exhaust gases.

There may also be other elements within the exhaust system, such as a muffler to reduce the exhaust noise or a water lock to stop the raw water from running back into the engine. These may be made of plastic and so need to be cooled, and they can easily become damaged if the cooling raw-water flow stops.

Plastic water lock

▲ Water lock connection to the engine and rubber exhaust pipe.

▲ Large fibreglass water lock.

TIP: EXHAUST SYSTEM CHECKS

Always check the exhaust system for damage if an engine has overheated due to a raw-water system failure. The exhaust pipe closest to the engine will be the most affected by heat damage and if this is OK then the rest of the system should be OK. Once you have fixed the cooling problem, though, do give the exhaust a visual check for water leaks once the engine has been restarted, especially around joins to the water locks and engine.

TIP: UNBLOCKING THE PEE HOLE

All outboards will have a 'pilot water hole', also called a 'pee hole', a tell-tale that tells you when the raw water is flowing properly through the system and you can see this clearly when the engine is running. These can become blocked and give the impression that water flow has ceased when in fact it hasn't. To unblock, simply take a paper clip, open it out and poke it up the tell-tale hole and this should get the flow starting again. If it doesn't start flowing again then you may well have a raw-water blockage. Check the raw-water inlets, which will be behind the propeller and below the anti-cavitation plate, on either side. If you still don't get any water coming out of the pilot water hole, it means you have an issue with the raw-water system flow and it is time to get a tow back home because the next step is to check the impeller, which as we know requires removal of the gearbox on an outboard engine. Continuous use of the engine without water flow can cause extensive damage.

Water coming out of the tell-tale hole on an outboard engine.

Jonathan says

With regard to overheating, it's amazing what can happen when what starts out as a simple problem isn't dealt with correctly.

I was called out to a sailing yacht where the engine had broken down due to overheating and as I went alongside, I was asked by the boat's skipper,

'Can you see any damage to the hull?'

A strange request, I thought, but I obliged. As I looked, there were no marks or scratches but I did see a bit of an indent about halfway along and this was quite a new 45-foot yacht, no more than a couple of years old.

When I said, 'Why do you ask?'

The chap said, 'Come on board. I'll explain.'

The boat was drifting at this point and so, to get it under control, we set the anchor. Going below, I saw that the L-shaped worktop in the galley area had been snapped in half and the cupboards were hanging off the wall.

'How did you manage to do that?' I asked curiously.

'Because we hadn't figured out how to put the sails up,' he said sheepishly.

'You're going to have to explain,' I said.

He said they were motoring along when the alarm for the engine went off and as they couldn't get the sails up, thought they had better go down to try and fix the engine (there were four of them on board). After about five minutes they heard an almighty crash. They had in fact run alongside a massive channel marker and side-swiped it.

'Why wasn't anybody up above on lookout?' I asked. Slowly, one by one, as each person saw the last was unable to rectify the issue, and thinking that they might be able to fix it, they had made their way down below, until they were all below decks. I'm sure that if given a bit more time before the collision, they would have all looked at each other and realised their mistake – no one was on watch. But alas, the channel marker came up all too quickly.

So, we needed to get the engine going, which had overheated. I thought this was probably due to a sea-water blockage. If you do have an engine overheat, the first thing you check is the strainer. So, I took the lid off to find nothing in the basket. However, there is supposed to be a black rubber seal around the lid, which was missing. I could see the seal in the bilge. I asked the skipper what happened when he picked the boat up. He explained that they thought they would do some engine checks as he'd attended some courses. So, he checked the raw-water strainer, then he replaced the lid. I pointed out that he had not paid enough attention because the seal had fallen off and he hadn't put it back on. With no seal, air would have been sucked into the top of the strainer and no raw water would be sucked into the system.

'When you started the engine up, you did not check to see if water was coming out of the exhaust?' Whenever you do anything with the water system or whenever you start the engine, you should always make sure you have water flow out of the exhaust. The thing about water flow and engine temperature is that the engine won't overheat straight away. It takes time for the engine to warm up, 10 to 15 minutes if you are under load, then once up to temperature it can take another 5 to 10 minutes after that before it starts to overheat. At this point the alarm at the helm will go off and this is what they had heard.

They would have motored for about 20 minutes at this point before the alarm sounded and this is without any water flow through the exhaust, just hot exhaust gases. So, we needed to check the exhaust pipe as well and we discovered that both the exhaust pipe and plastic water lock had melted. As a result of this we had to check the impeller and we found that this had been completely destroyed and all the vanes had broken off. In fact, the friction of the impeller turning without any water flowing through had created such a heat that the sticker on the front of the impeller housing had burnt off completely. Obviously, we couldn't do too much with it – there is no point changing the impeller when the exhaust is damaged – and as we didn't have the right exhaust available to fit, all we could do was tow them back.

It turned out it was a charter boat. They had completed an RYA Day Skipper course four years previously, which allowed them to charter. On the way in they asked me if, once it was fixed, I could show them how to put the sails up. I said, 'I'll speak to the charter company and recommend in fact that you don't take it

back out again, because obviously you can neither look after the engine, nor put the sails up, so I really don't think you should be using it!'

The damage that resulted from that initial mistake of not spotting that the seal had fallen out of the lid for the strainer and not checking that water was coming out of the exhaust was extensive and expensive – raw-water pipework, impeller and exhaust needing to be replaced, and then of course there was the structural damage to the boat, the topsides and the galley. The boat would have to be lifted and a surveyor called to check the hull.

Moral of the story: carry out your regular engine checks, ensuring they have been done properly, and never leave a boat without a watch keeper. The International Regulations for Preventing Collisions at Sea Rule 5 states:

'Every vessel shall at all times maintain a proper lookout by sight and hearing as well as by all available means appropriate in the prevailing circumstances and conditions so as to make a full appraisal of the situation and of the risk of collision.'

▲ *Hitting a buoy like this port-hand marker will seriously damage your boat and increase your insurance premiums.*

6 Air systems

Why is air so important to your engine? Because fuel will only burn if it is given oxygen and air contains oxygen.

How does your engine access air?

It sucks air in on the inlet stroke via an air inlet on the engine. The air comes in via an air filter, through the inlet manifold, past the intake valves and into the cylinder.

◆ Do we need to change air filters regularly?

This depends on the engine. We need to check air filters regularly. Most air filters have paper elements that you change. Some of the older and smaller diesel engines might not have an element at all. Some filters are just perforated pieces of metal, which are designed to prevent larger pieces of debris entering the engine; some are made of foam. Marine engines don't suffer from the same dirt and dust issues that car engines suffer from because there is no road dirt, dust or debris in the air in an engine bay.

▲ A metal filter.

The route air takes through the filter and into the cylinder

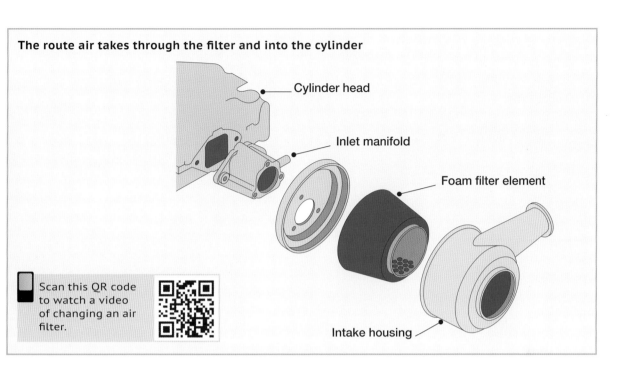

Cylinder head

Inlet manifold

Foam filter element

Intake housing

Scan this QR code to watch a video of changing an air filter.

Air intake and air filter

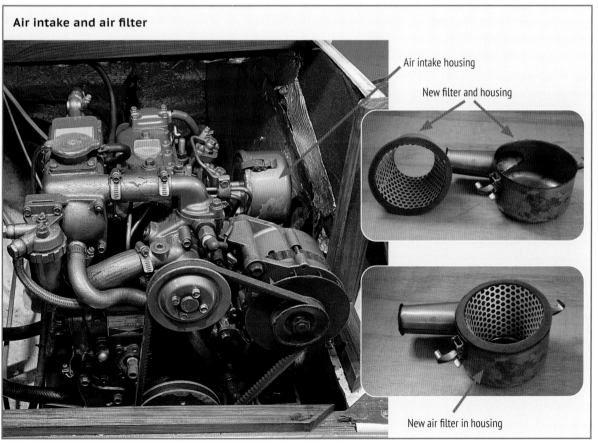

Air intake housing

New filter and housing

New air filter in housing

▲ *A foam filter.*

Petrol breather pipes

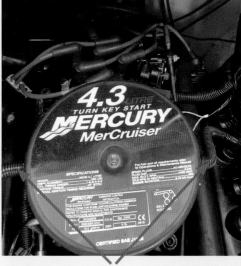

▲ Mercury 4.3 litre petrol engine

Engine breathers allowing the moisture from the hot oil vapours to be sucked directly into the air filter

Volvo Penta TAMD 122 crankcase filters

Crankcase filters   Oil pipe to drain sump   Air filter

As the crankcase vapours enter the filters, the oil within the vapour is collected and then returns to the sump. The remaining vapours exit the filter holes and are sucked back into the engine by the air filter, to be burnt off.

HOW MUCH AIR DOES AN ENGINE NEED?

Engines require a great deal of air. To work out how much air they need, consider the following: A 2-litre normally aspirated engine running at 2,000 revs per minute will suck 2 cubic metres of air in per minute. That's 120 cubic metres per hour.

What is 120 cubic metres in terms of a physical space? Well, a space measuring 10 metres long by 4 metres wide by 3 metres high will contain 120 cubic metres of air, the size of a small bungalow. And the 2-litre engine needs this much every hour at only 2,000rpm. Just imagine now what a 4-litre turbocharged engine at 4,000rpm would be using, it could be up to 4 times as much, about the same as a good-sized detached house. All this air from just the small amount of space around the engine, the size of a doll's house!

Common causes of air system problems

◆ Exhaust leaks

Normally when an air filter gets blocked it is the result of an exhaust leak. The engine sucks in the exhaust air, which is dirty and clogs the filter.

◆ Failure in the oil breathing system

First, what is the oil breathing system?

There is a good deal of air in an engine. There is air around the crankshaft, which is suspended on its bearings with the oil sump directly below it. There is air at the top of the engine where the valves go up and down. And this air has moisture within it and when the air gets hot it will want to evaporate but if it can't escape, it will become trapped in the top of the engine. The moisture in the air will mix with the oil and create a creaminess – you can see this emulsion of water and oil if you take the oil cap off the engine. So, to allow the air and the moisture to escape, a pipe is fitted to the top of the engine.

This pipe is normally connected to a crankcase breather, which is something that needs to be checked when the engine is serviced and which is right next to the air filter.

WHAT DOES THE BLAST OF BLACK SMOKE FROM THE EXHAUST WHEN STARTING THE ENGINE INDICATE?

This indicates that the engine cylinders are cold and therefore for the first couple of turns of the engine you end up with more fuel to the cylinders than oxygen and the fuel will burn as black smoke. As soon as the cylinder temperature increases, the black smoke will reduce and then disappear.

When the weather is cold, the engine will create more black smoke than when it is warm, because the engine has to work a little bit harder to get the cylinders to the correct temperature to burn the fuel, on initial start up.

If black smoke at the start up is a new issue or is getting progressively worse, then it will indicate one of the following:

- The engine cold start system is defective – diesel engines can use 'glow plugs', which pre-heat the air before combustion. Or the 'choke' on a petrol carburettor engine requires adjustment.
- The engine cylinders on a diesel are getting low on compression due to worn piston rings or valves not sealing correctly so not enough heat is being generated from the compression. And a petrol engine that is low on compression may not ignite the fuel fully from the spark. In any event, there is something wrong with these engines and a compression check should be carried out. On an older engine with many hours on the clock, low compression is to be expected.
- Too much fuel is being introduced to the engine when cold. This could be a defective fuel injector that no longer vaporises fuel in a neat pattern or leaks in between combustion cycles.

The crankcase breather allows air and moisture to return to the engine via the air filter and the oil which is heavier than air, to drop down into the oil sump. The crankcase breather prevents moisture from evaporating within the engine room and leaving an oily residue and a bad oily smell.

Older engines don't normally have a crankcase breather. They usually have a pipe that goes straight from the top of the engine to the air filter, which means that the evaporation, the moisture, is not filtered and the air filter will clog up more quickly than an air filter with a crankcase breather fitted.

So, we need to check the air filter on older engines and the air filter in the crankcase breather on more modern engines to ensure that the filter is not blocked.

◆ Not enough air in the engine bay

Engine rooms or bays are generally small and do not contain enough air to 'feed' the engine. Many engine rooms will have fans and some sort of air ducting that allows air into the engine bay and which allows the air inside to circulate. Yacht engines tend to have very small engine rooms.

Engine rooms will often have fans to give the engine that much needed air and to supplement the fact that air vents and ducts only work well when a boat is travelling at speed.

Most motorboat engines therefore have fans, which are designed:

1. to give the engine plenty of air
2. to push air through the engine bay to make sure any combustible fumes are extracted
3. to provide plenty of fresh oxygenated air in the engine bay for the engine start. This is why the engine bay fans come on before the engines are started. This is especially important when starting an engine from cold and for petrol inboard engines.

◆ What happens when your engine doesn't get enough air?

Not enough air means not enough oxygen to mix with the diesel and the result is diesel that is being burned inefficiently. An indicator of this is black smoke coming out of the exhaust and there will be a sooty deposit on the water. Then you will lose power as the engine revs reduce. You may reach a point where the engine revs will remain stable. This indicates that at this level of revs the engine is getting enough air.

But try and rev beyond this and without the extra air required the engine will simply not pick up the revs. It will produce a lot of black smoke and carbon deposits within the engine and exhaust will build up. This can do permanent damage to the engine and at the very least reduce its performance.

Air is as important as fuel for an engine.

If you have black smoke coming out of the exhaust, check the air filter, in case this is blocked. Also make sure that any engine room fans, if fitted, are working.

There are many reasons why an engine will have black smoke coming out of the exhaust. See 'Know your smoke' in Chapter 12, How to troubleshoot a breakdown.

Jonathan says

I was once called by someone who was on a chartered racing yacht, quite small, about 30 feet, which had a small engine, probably around 20 horsepower. It seems with sailing yachts that engines are almost an afterthought. In fact, when they started fitting engines to yachts, they were described as auxiliary engines, just enough to get the boat in and out of the harbour.

I was called out because a charter boat had lost power coming down the river and had ended up on the harbourmaster's pontoon, where I met up with the skipper. I had a look around the engine, which started up perfectly with no problems, so I had another look around it. I took the side covers off but I couldn't find out what the problem had been. This was strange because the engine was running perfectly fine. However, I noticed that the engine was enclosed in a small space with panelling all around it, the companionway stairs in front of it, the walls either side and at the back. These walls were covered with very thick insulation, which came to within just a few inches of the engine, so there wasn't much air space in there at all. And as I looked above the engine, there were two plastic conduits coming down and one had a fan in it, which I noticed wasn't working. It looked like the wire had broken off the back but upon closer inspection it looked as though it had in fact been cut.

I telephoned the charter company, who said that the last person to use the boat informed them that they had heard a funny noise coming from the engine room and discovered that it was the fan motor, so rather than fix it they just cut the wire to it to stop the noise. They left it like that, so when the next people had gone to use the boat, they had the problem that with all the side panels on, the steps in place and the engine being completely enclosed, the conduit on its own wasn't allowing enough air into the engine room for the engine to run at full speed. So, as the boat was travelling down the River Hamble, it was becoming starved of air and just kept slowing down, simply because the fan was not working and blowing in the required amount of air.

Although the fan motor would have to be replaced, the simple solution in the short term was to take one of the side panels off the engine room, which would then allow all the air needed to get to the engine. And this did the trick. Cutting the wire to stop the fan resulted in the engine being starved of air. You wouldn't believe how much air an engine needs to be able to work (see 'How much air does an engine need?').

7 Lubrication system

Why lubricating is important

Lubrication is what keeps the internal metal components of the engine apart from each other.

The crankshaft is held in suspension by the main bearings, which are flat pieces of metal shaped to the curves of the crankshaft. The oil pump sucks the oil from the sump, then pumps it in at high pressure to these bearings so that when the crankshaft turns it is kept away from the metal of the bearings by the oil pressure alone. Holes are milled through the crankshaft to allow the oil pressure to reach the big end bearings of the connecting rod, which is attached to the piston. The crankshaft is effectively turning in a sleeve of oil. The oil lubricates the parts and allows the engine to run cooler than it would if the metal parts were touching.

The oil comes out of the sides of the bearings, through a small gap that is designed to maintain the pressure in the bearing, before going back into the sump. Then it will be filtered and go round again. Any debris from wear and tear on the metal of the crankshaft and bearings will be carried away by the oil and will go into the sump to be trapped by the filter.

Oil is also pumped under pressure to the camshaft bearings and the hydraulic tappets. If pushrods are fitted, they are hollow and allow the oil to travel up

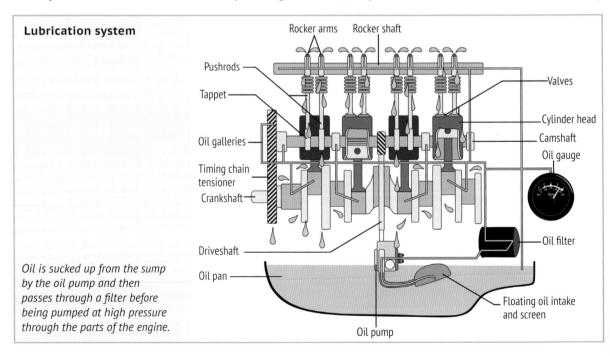

Lubrication system

Rocker arms   Rocker shaft

Pushrods

Tappet

Oil galleries

Timing chain tensioner

Crankshaft

Driveshaft

Oil pan

Oil pump

Valves

Cylinder head

Camshaft

Oil gauge

Oil filter

Floating oil intake and screen

Oil is sucked up from the sump by the oil pump and then passes through a filter before being pumped at high pressure through the parts of the engine.

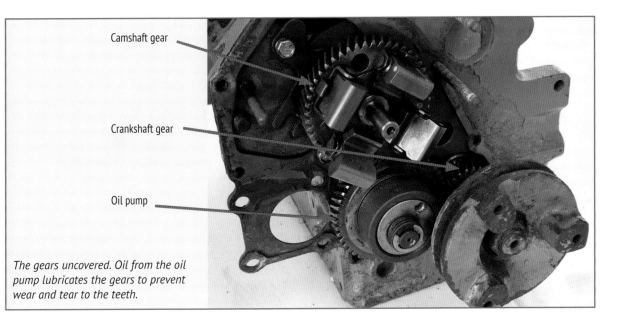

Camshaft gear

Crankshaft gear

Oil pump

The gears uncovered. Oil from the oil pump lubricates the gears to prevent wear and tear to the teeth.

through them to the rocker arms and valve springs, helping lubricate the moving parts in the cylinder head.

Oil is also sprayed up into the bottom of the cylinders, where the pistons go up and down, and this also lubricates the piston rings, which in turn lubricate the side wall of the cylinder. And oil gets pumped up to the valves on the top of the cylinder and lubricates the valve stems.

Oil is used to lubricate fuel pumps. As diesel is actually a refined oil, this is often sufficient lubrication on its own, but occasionally they need more lubrication and this is provided by oil. The oil is a specific type designed to lubricate the moving parts of the pump and will have its own oil level which can be checked, and an oil drain to replace it.

Gears connecting the crankshaft and the camshaft will require oil to prevent wear and tear on the teeth.

Camchains and cambelts

Sometimes the connection between crankshaft and camshaft is by a camchain or a cambelt. If the connection is via a camchain, this will need to be lubricated to prevent it wearing or corroding. A cambelt – made of rubber – does not need to be lubricated but will require changing at set intervals – after five years on older engines, after ten years on modern engines. You can tell if you have a camchain or a cambelt on your engine because an engine with a camchain will have a metal cover over the chain and one with a cambelt will have a plastic cover over the belt.

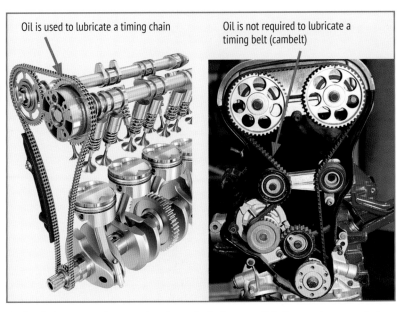

Oil is used to lubricate a timing chain

Oil is not required to lubricate a timing belt (cambelt)

▲ *Cambelts are used on overhead camshafts because it is the most economical way of making the connection between crankshaft and camshaft.*

Gearbox lubrication

The gearbox has its own lubrication system and the oil needs to be checked regularly and topped up where required.

Most marine gearboxes have a dipstick to check the oil level. Gearbox oils don't degrade to the same degree as engine oils because there is no combustion going on and you don't get the blackness you get in engine oils. Gearbox oil should really stay the same colour as when new and you want the oil to remain as clean as possible. Gearboxes do have a service interval but this is generally every two years rather than annually. Or it may be that you just keep checking the oil until you decide that it no longer looks clean and needs to be changed. Ideally, you should change it while it is clean.

Most marine gearboxes have two gears: one forward and one reverse, with neutral in between. These use a cone clutch. This is a conical-shaped cylinder, which moves one way into forward gear before locking into place, back again to neutral and then the other way to lock into reverse. These are simple gearboxes that require no oil filter and gearboxes on small engines may need only about a ¼ litre of oil.

Gearboxes can get a good deal more complicated and you can have hydraulic gearboxes, which go in

and out of gear hydraulically using a pressurised oil system, which requires an oil filter and which needs to be changed periodically. Some gearboxes can be electronic. So, instead of using a mechanical cable to change gear, they use solenoids to push them in and out of gear. The clutches within hydraulically operated gearboxes differ from the more basic cone-clutch systems and as a result require different grades and temperature ranges of oil.

Gearbox oils range from the same multigrade oil you put in the engine through to a single grade oil or red automatic transmission fluid that you also get in cars, depending on the complexity of the gearbox. So, it's important to find out what sort of oil your gearbox uses.

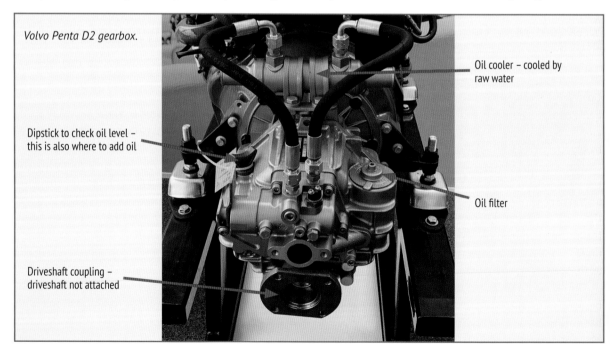

Volvo Penta D2 gearbox.

Oil cooler – cooled by raw water

Dipstick to check oil level – this is also where to add oil

Oil filter

Driveshaft coupling – driveshaft not attached

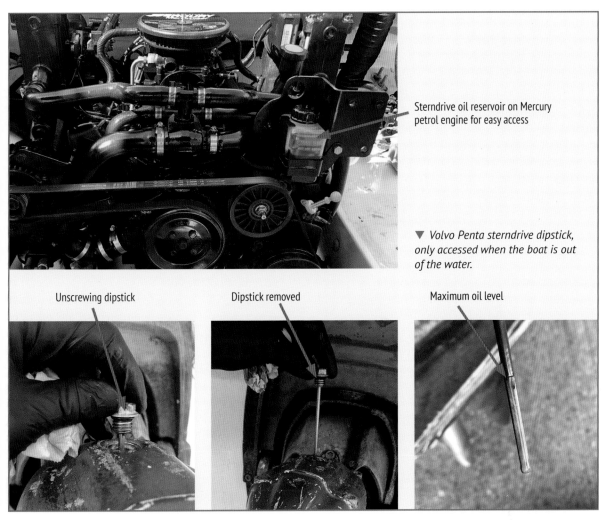

Sterndrive oil reservoir on Mercury petrol engine for easy access

▼ *Volvo Penta sterndrive dipstick, only accessed when the boat is out of the water.*

Unscrewing dipstick

Dipstick removed

Maximum oil level

◆ The colour of gearbox oil

Gearbox oils change colour for various reasons, the most common reason being water ingress. Whereas some gearboxes are what is called 'stand alone', in that they do not need to be cooled, other gearboxes can be cooled by raw water passing through them via a small heat exchanger.

Some gearboxes are actually underwater. Sail drives on yachts have the bottom part of the gearbox underwater, for example. The gearbox on a sterndrive is underwater and the same goes for outboard engines where the gearbox is situated on the bottom half of the engine where the propeller is attached and is underwater when the engine is in the down position. All underwater gearboxes are subject to water ingress and thus emulsification as the water and oil mix together.

Checking gearbox oil levels on sail drives and most sterndrives needs to be done when the boat is out of the water. There are some sterndrives that have oil reservoirs inside the boat for checking the level and topping it up – Mercury and Volvo are examples.

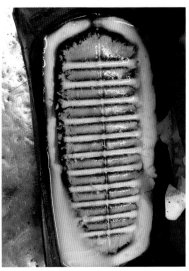

▲ *Emulsified oil.*

If you spot that the oil is becoming 'hazy' in a sail drive or sterndrive this is an indication that you have water in the oil. It has not yet become creamy or emulsified but it is on its way and the water leak needs to be stopped and the oil changed. The leak might be the result of a perished gasket, or a worn or damaged lip seal. Gearboxes are made in sections and there will be seals and gaskets where they are bolted together. There are also lip seals underwater on sterndrives on the output shafts where the propellers attach and where the gear selectors connect to the shaft. Seals are subject to normal wear and tear but then you can also get fishing line caught round the propeller or the shaft on sail drives, sterndrives and outboards, where it can work its way into the seal. Whatever the cause of the water ingress, it needs to be checked and rectified.

Gearbox oil can also turn black, like engine oil. It shouldn't, but it tells you that small metal particles are in the oil, the result of bearing wear generally or, if it has clutches, which transfer from forward to reverse, a sign that the clutch is slipping. If you see the gearbox oil starting to blacken, it is a sign of excess wear in the gearbox.

Keep an eye on the quality of the oil because it is always the quality of the oil that indicates if there is a problem.

Look after your lubrication system

Your lubrication system should become part of your regular engine checks. If you haven't been to the boat for a while, you need to:
- Check the engine oil level and quality.
- Check gearbox oil level and quality – *sterndrive gearboxes, being underwater, can only be checked when the boat is out of the water.*
- Check steering fluid level and quality if you have a hydraulic steering system.
- Check your power trim oil level and quality, if fitted.
- Check your trim tab oil level and quality, if fitted.
- Check supercharger oil level and quality, if fitted.
- Check for any oil leaks and identify the source and type of oil to discover what system is leaking.
- Always keep a supply of all these types of oil on board for topping up.
- Keep your engine and bilges clean so leaks can be easily identified.

- Change any oil systems at the manufacturer's recommended intervals to prevent excessive wear and tear.

By checking levels and keeping an eye on them throughout the season, you will be able to spot any issues before they become a major problem and something fails.

Changing the engine oil and oil filter

Check your engine operator's manual but essentially these are the steps.
1. Warm the engine up to its operating temperature to thin the oil, which will make it easier to extract.
2. Remove the oil cap and dipstick to allow air in and aid removal of the oil.
3. Attach your oil extraction device to the oil extraction point as advised by the engine manufacturer – possibly the dipstick tube or a special port.
4. Suck the oil out.
5. Change the oil filter.
6. Top up the oil to the correct level.
7. Run the engine for 10 seconds and re-check the oil level.
8. Re-fit the oil cap.

▼ *Oil filter and filter wrench.*

Scan this QR code to watch a video on changing the oil and oil filter.

Jonathan says

Checking your oil levels and quality is very important and not doing regular checks can end in excessive wear and tear followed by complete failure.

I am reminded of a workboat I used to operate when I was at Sea Start. It had two 150hp outboards and we used it to attend broken-down boats, fixing them if possible or towing them in if necessary. The engines on this boat required servicing every 100 hours. It was the summer, our busiest time of year for attending breakdowns, when the boat was on the water all day every day and soon the engine hours tot up.

The day the boat was scheduled for a service turned out to be one of my busiest. In fact, between Chichester, Poole, back to the Ise of Wight, up to Southampton, back to Hayling Island and finally across to Lymington before returning to Hamble, I must have covered 120 miles over about 12 hours.

The engines seemed to be running perfectly throughout the day, though, so we decided to get the boat lifted for its service the next day.

All seemed fine as we started servicing the engine, until we drained the gearbox oils. On one engine the oil was still a lovely, clear, golden yellow, just as it should be. On the other engine, however, it was ever so slightly different, it was even clearer! In fact, all that came out was completely clean sea water. I had never seen this before. Oil contamination is not uncommon but in mixing with water the oil would be emulsified and creamy in texture. Here, all we had in the gearbox was water, no oil.

Amazingly, there had been no issues with the gearbox. It had worked fine. The bearings were quiet with no excessive wear or noise.

Conscious that we had emptied a gearbox full of sea water, which would now be corroding the internal components, we drained the water out and flushed it through thoroughly with fresh water, then again with a light oil and then refilled it with gear oil completely and sent the gearbox away to be dismantled and checked. Surprisingly, it was found to be still in great shape and we soon had it back, refitted it and all has been well with the gearbox since.

I suppose the lesson here is to do regular checks and carry out a service at the correct time. Don't put it off as you never know when a problem will occur and sometimes there are no symptoms at all when the issue first occurs. If we hadn't done the service when we did, the gearbox would undoubtedly have failed. So, spotting it early by doing the service will have saved a lot of time and effort, not to mention the cost of rebuilding a gearbox. And of course, it avoided the 'breakdown' boat from breaking down. That could have been embarrassing.

8 Electrical system

The basic electrical system

Any marine electrical system starts with the battery or batteries. There are two types of battery on a boat:

1. A heavy-duty, engine start battery that delivers a punch or rather a high current to turn the engine over, where the power consumption of the battery is replaced almost immediately by the alternator.

2. A domestic battery that delivers a constant and lower current to power the boat's electrical systems such as lighting, navigation instruments, fresh-water pumps. This will be a deep-cycle battery that can be discharged to 50 per cent and then charged up to full again and again, charging taking twice as long to replace as the time it took to use up the charge.

All batteries have a positive or live terminal (normally red) and a negative earth terminal (normally black). Battery terminals always have one terminal with a + symbol (positive) and the other a – symbol (negative) next to it. The positive terminal is normally larger than the negative terminal to help prevent attaching the cables the wrong way round.

SOME BASIC ELECTRICAL TERMS

Charge (volts): Charge is rated in volts and the electrical system on a boat is generally 12-volt DC (direct current) but you can also have 24-volt DC systems, which use 2 x 12-volt batteries wired together in 'series' and acting as one single 24V battery.

Current (amps): Current, measured in amps, is the flow of electricity. The more current you send down a cable, the more power can be transferred between the power source (the battery) and what you want to power (eg engine starter motor).

Power (watts): Electrical power is rated in watts, which are volts multiplied by the current in amps, so 40 amps from a 12-volt battery gives you (40A × 12V) 480 watts.

Note: The more current you send down a wire, the thicker that wire needs to be. If you restrict the flow by using cables that are not thick enough to carry the current, you cause the cable to heat up and you find that you lose power, with a lower power output at the end of the cable than at the start.

However, you can reduce the current by increasing the charge and so if you were to use a 24V battery to get your power of 480W you would find that your current had reduced to 20A - 480W ÷ 24V = 20A. By increasing the voltage you decrease the current.

This is why larger boats will often have 24V systems, because their electric cables run long distances. Were they to use a 12V system, the current running down the cable would be considerable so they would need to be thick and would generate heat. By running a 24V system they can halve the current and reduce cable thickness and thus weight and heat.

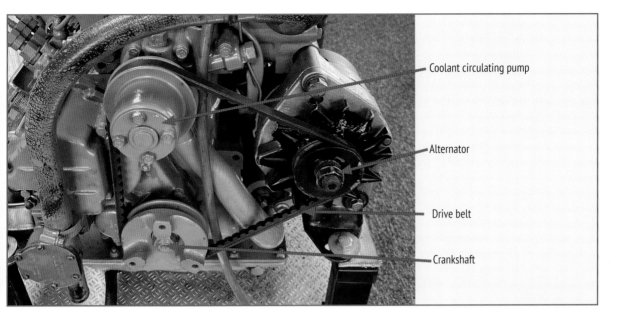

Coolant circulating pump

Alternator

Drive belt

Crankshaft

◆ The engine start battery

This connects via the positive terminal on the battery to

1. a battery isolator switch, then
2. to the back of the starter motor solenoid, then
3. to the ignition switch, then
4. to the engine instrument panel.

The negative wire of the battery generally goes to the engine block and the block then becomes an earth/ negative connection or common earth for all electrical units fitted to the engine.

Some boats' systems differ in that they do not use the engine block as a common earth and so every individual item that needs to be earthed must be earthed separately on its own. On some systems the negative or earth cable is actually switched, so it may have its own battery on/off isolator switch. If this is the case then for identification purposes, positive battery switches are normally red and negative ones black.

When you turn on the ignition, the engine instruments will come on. A further turn of the ignition will activate the starter motor, which will turn over the engine and the engine will start. If you have a diesel engine and it has glow plugs fitted, they should be operated for about 10 seconds before you turn the key to activate the starter motor, to aid cold starting. When the engine is warm you do not need to pre-heat the cylinders with the glow plugs.

The engine will have on it an alternator, which is a battery charger. This battery charger is driven from the crankshaft by a drive belt and via a voltage regulator charges both the engine battery and the domestic battery.

◆ The difference between a heavy-duty battery and a domestic battery

Every battery is made up of separate cells. A 12-volt battery comprises six 2.1-volt cells that added together total 12.6 volts, which represents a fully charged battery.

Each individual cell is a battery in itself and within the battery cells are a number of metal plates, which are immersed in an electrolyte – sulphuric acid. The more plates there are in a cell, the greater the surface area, the greater current you can generate within that cell.

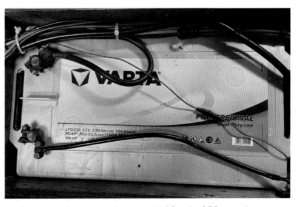

▲ Domestic battery – deep-cycle 12 volt, 230 amp hours.

BATTERY CHARGE LEVELS

Voltage	State of charge
12.60+	100%
12.50	90%
12.42	80%
12.32	70%
12.20	60%
12.06	50%
11.90	40%
11.75	30%
11.58	20%
11.31	10%
10.50	0%

Near or on your domestic switch panel you should have a battery indicator for the domestic battery and may have an indicator for the engine start battery – otherwise this will be on the engine instrument panel.

They are not always very accurate and so, having checked this, you should check the battery terminals with a multimeter and note the difference for the future – the difference is the degree of error in the battery indicator.

Be careful not to connect anything between the positive and negative terminals, certainly not you, nor any metal item.

Battery indicator reading about 13.5+ volts for engine start battery

Battery measured at 13.73 volts – all OK

Battery indicator reading 13 volts for domestic battery

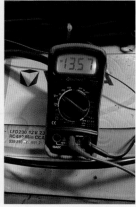

Battery measured at 13.57 volts so battery indicator under-reading slightly

Battery indicator reading 27 volts for engine start battery

Battery measured at 26.7 volts so indicator more or less spot on

Battery indicator reading 28.5 volts for domestic battery

Battery measured at 27.9 volts so battery indicator over-reading slightly

▲ *Heavy-duty engine start battery - 12 volt, 95 amp hours, 830 amp cold cranking charge.*

A heavy-duty battery, which needs to deliver a large current for a short time to start the engine, has a great many plates in the cells. As a result, the plates are fairly thin.

A domestic deep-cycle battery, which is designed to provide less current but over a longer period, has fewer plates per cell and these plates are thicker than those in a heavy-duty battery, for good reason. The process of discharging a battery and then charging it up again degrades the plates and so a deep-cycle battery can stand many discharges and recharges before wearing out.

So heavy-duty batteries should be used for starting engines and domestic deep-cycle batteries should be used for domestic systems. However, if the deep-cycle battery is powerful enough and can turn the engine over then you can use it to start an engine.

You shouldn't use a heavy-duty battery as a domestic battery for any length of time because the thin plates will decay quickly with the constant discharging and recharging that is the pattern for domestic use.

Batteries need to be matched to the job they are required to do. People often make the mistake of thinking that as the engine start battery needs to deliver the most power, it will be the larger of the two batteries. In truth, this is not generally the case.

For example, a yacht with a 20 to 30hp engine would need a heavy-duty battery rated at 85 amp hours with a cold cranking current of say 500 amps to be able to start the engine over a period of only a couple of seconds. (Cold cranking being the rating required to turn the engine over when cold.)

WHAT IS AN AMP HOUR?

1 amp hour (Ah) is power consumption of 1 amp for 1 hour.

Take your navigation lights – side lights port and starboard and stern light. If they are each rated at 3 amps, there being 3 of them, they will require 9 amps of power every hour. If you had a 250Ah battery and were sailing (not charging the batteries) you could run these three lights for 250Ah ÷ 9A = 27.78 hours, before the 250Ah battery was completely discharged. That is one reason why yachts under 20 metres make use of a tricolour light at the masthead. This is a sectored light in place of the port, starboard and stern lights that uses just one bulb. If that is a 3Ah bulb then you could run this for 250Ah ÷ 3A = 83.33 hours before the 250Ah battery would have discharged completely.

Yachts sailing offshore will tend to run their engines once in 24 hours, as a result, in order to charge their batteries. Motorboats don't have to worry as they are charging their batteries all the time when motoring.

THE RIGHT BATTERY FOR THE JOB

In an ideal world we should use a heavy-duty battery for engine starting and a deep-cycle battery for the domestic electrics. But you will often find boats with 2 x deep-cycle batteries or 2 x heavy-duty batteries, or selector switches that allow them to choose which battery they will use for what purpose. A deep-cycle battery will start an engine if it is powerful enough and then there are dual-purpose batteries. At the end of the day, the demands on the battery from an engine are very different from those of the domestic electrical system and it is best to have batteries that are suited to each role – a heavy-duty and a deep-cycle.

The domestic deep-cycle battery on this boat might have to power everything from the Eberspacher hot-air heater to the navigation instruments, lights, radar, autopilot and fridge and so might need to be rated for a 250 amp hour life, because it will be operating over a prolonged period.

◆ Wiring for a domestic deep-cycle battery

The positive and negative from the domestic deep-cycle battery will go to a fused switch panel. It is here that you switch on the power to whatever instrument you wish to use in the boat, from navigation instruments and navigation lights to the fridge and the domestic lights.

▲ A switch panel on a 35-foot sailing boat.

▲ A switch panel on a 23-metre motor yacht.

◆ Wiring diagrams

It is worth understanding how the electricity goes round the system, especially when it comes to fault-finding when you will have to check the voltage at certain points to establish what is happening.

So here are the sorts of wiring setups you will have on a boat.

▼ This is the sort of wiring you will generally have on a sports cruiser or a RIB, although they can also have a domestic battery to run sound systems, cool boxes and so forth when at anchor without running down the engine battery.

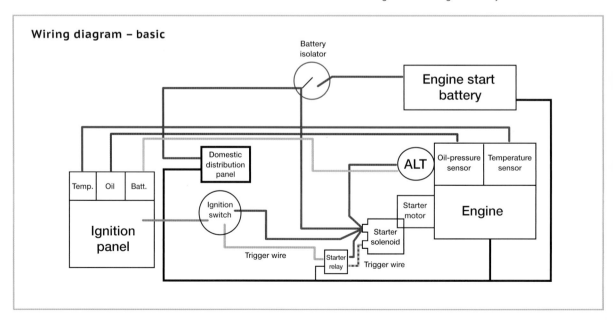

Wiring diagram – basic

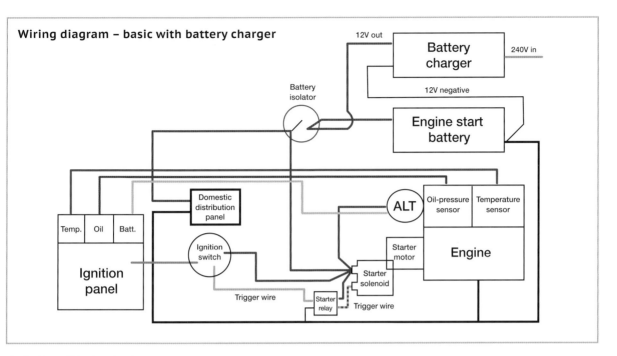

Wiring diagram – basic with battery charger

12V out

Battery charger

240V in

12V negative

Battery isolator

Engine start battery

Domestic distribution panel

ALT

Oil-pressure sensor

Temperature sensor

Engine

Temp. | Oil | Batt.

Ignition switch

Starter motor

Ignition panel

Starter solenoid

Trigger wire

Starter relay

Trigger wire

▲ *And here it is showing how a 240-volt battery charger is wired into the system.*

Yours may not be exactly the same as these diagrams because people add things and change things over time and these diagrams do not include equipment such as a windlass, which will be fused separately from the domestic system and have its own isolator switch.

Other common wiring setups may include a battery selector switch, a battery charger, or a diode splitter and separate isolator switches for each battery. The advantage of a diode splitter over a selector switch is that the diode splitter sorts out battery charging for you. With a selector switch you have to decide which batteries you want to charge, 1, 2 or both and turn the switch accordingly – and that's where people forget. Suddenly you find that one or both of the batteries have lost their charge because the selector switch was in the wrong place. A diode splitter removes the opportunity for human error.

With a rotary control like this, you need to be careful. Assuming that '1' is the engine battery, switch to this to start the engine. Then when it is running switch to 'All', now both '1' the engine battery and '2' the domestic battery will be charged. When you turn the engine off, say you are moored or at anchor, turn the control to '2' for the domestic battery. Now charge will be taken from the domestic battery only. If you leave the switch on 'All' while you have the engine off, charge can come from both batteries and you can run down the engine battery. Then, if the engine won't start, you will be unable to charge either of the batteries.

◀ *Separate switches.*

Another system for linking the engine start battery and the domestic battery and charging them both is with a split charge relay. Being a relay, this needs power to turn it on – whereas a diode does not – and when on it will link the two batteries and allow the charge from the alternator to reach them.

We have shown just two 12-volt batteries, a heavy-duty engine start and a deep-cycle domestic in these diagrams. You may have several domestic batteries and more than one engine start battery on your boat. You will wire your batteries in parallel, assuming you require more capacity at 12 volts.

Some systems will have an additional battery switch which can be used in an emergency to start the engine if the engine battery is flat or failed. It will connect the domestic battery directly to the engine battery and 'jump start' the engine.

◆ Checking voltages

For this you need a voltmeter but put 'voltmeter' into the internet and you get an array of instruments that look complicated enough to, well, to land a rover

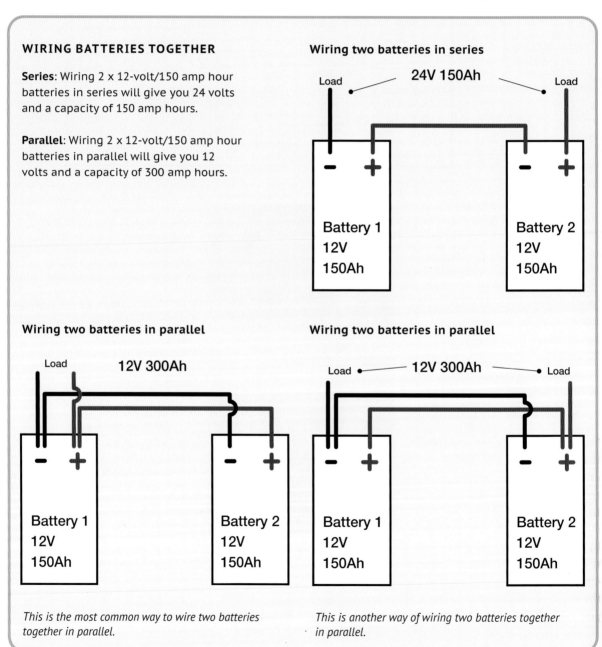

WIRING BATTERIES TOGETHER

Series: Wiring 2 x 12-volt/150 amp hour batteries in series will give you 24 volts and a capacity of 150 amp hours.

Parallel: Wiring 2 x 12-volt/150 amp hour batteries in parallel will give you 12 volts and a capacity of 300 amp hours.

Wiring two batteries in series

24V 150Ah

Load

Load

Battery 1
12V
150Ah

Battery 2
12V
150Ah

Wiring two batteries in parallel

Load   12V 300Ah

Battery 1
12V
150Ah

Battery 2
12V
150Ah

This is the most common way to wire two batteries together in parallel.

Wiring two batteries in parallel

Load   12V 300Ah   Load

Battery 1
12V
150Ah

Battery 2
12V
150Ah

This is another way of wiring two batteries together in parallel.

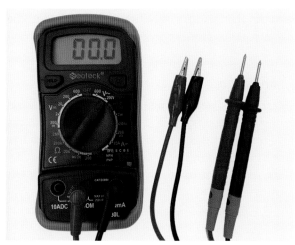

▲ *Voltmeter with handy crocodile clips. I find it hard to maintain contact with two probes at the same time and being able to clip one end is useful.*

on Mars. But don't worry, these are multimeters and they include a voltmeter.

If the meter reads 12.6 volts, you are in business. If it reads 12.0 volts, either the battery is fairly well discharged and needs to be charged or it is near the end of its life.

◆ The engine starting sequence

The order of things when turning on the ignition is as follows:

1. The ignition switch turns on the starter relay.
2. The starter relay turns on the starter solenoid.
3. The starter solenoid turns on the starter motor.
4. The starter motor turns the crankshaft, which starts the engine.

The starter motor needs a good deal of power to turn the engine over, between 150 and 350 amps depending on the size of the engine. And so rather than running thick cables capable of carrying this high load from the battery all the way to the ignition and back to the starter motor, a starter relay is used. This is activated by a small current from the ignition, which in turn then activates the starter solenoid, requiring about 4 times the power of the starter relay, and this powers the starter motor, which requires around 10 times the power of the solenoid.

This then keeps the thick cables required to carry a heavy load to a minimum – a short run from starter solenoid to starter motor – and allows the cabling from battery to ignition to be narrow gauge as the ignition is only sending a signal to the starter relay at around 5 amps.

Mind you, not all boats have a starter relay, some just have a starter solenoid. You will find the starter solenoid attached to the starter motor and the starter relay nearby.

So, if the engine doesn't start for any reason, you need to make sure that each part of the starting process is getting juice – volts and amps. Now, before you get out your voltmeter, as you will discover in Chapter 12 How to troubleshoot a breakdown, you test the easy things first, those things you can reach easily or in this case those things you can see and hear. Because observing and listening will help you identify what's going on and can tell you immediately where the problem lies.

For example, when starting the engine:

Is the ignition light on?
If you turn the ignition on and the ignition light comes on then you have power to the ignition switch. No light? Then you need to check the ignition fuse and if you are getting 12V to the ignition switch.

Rapid clicking
If you turn the key and hear a rapid clicking sound, this tells you that the battery is flat, or that the connections from battery to starter relay/solenoid/motor are loose. Check the battery voltage and that the wires are all making a good connection.

One click
If you turn the key and you hear one quite quiet click, this is the sound of the starter relay. It is supposed to make the connection to send the signal to the starter solenoid but somehow it is not making that connection. It may be that it has corroded. A light tap with a finger or a spanner might free it. If you cannot free it then connecting the live and the trigger wire (see diagram on page 94) on the back of the starter solenoid will start the engine – assuming there is nothing wrong with the starter solenoid. Just make the connection ideally using a wire with suitable connections at each end and a push button switch in the middle. Do be careful that none of your clothing is anywhere near the drive belt or other

moving parts of the engine that will start turning the minute the engine has started.

Loud clunk

If you turn the key and you hear a loud clunk then this is the plate in the starter solenoid that has jammed. Again, try tapping the starter solenoid to see if you can free it. And also give the starter motor a little tap. If none of this works then the issue is with the starter solenoid and starter motor and you need to call an engineer.

A little about what is happening with the starter relay, starter solenoid and starter motor.

A starter relay is a switch. It relays a small current from the ignition to cause a much larger current from the battery to operate the starter solenoid on the starter motor.

The starter solenoid is activated by the current from the starter relay and has a plunger within it that closes contacts that switch on the starter motor and it also moves a pinion gear to engage the flywheel.

◆ What does a fuse do and where will you find them?

A fuse is just a weak link and the degree of its weakness is shown on the casing. A 3-amp fuse will blow if the load through it exceeds 3 amps. They are a fail-safe in case of a fault with the appliance or a 'short' where for some reason, corrosion usually, the plastic or rubber coating of a wire has perished, or where corrosion at the terminals causes the positive and negative wires to come into contact, which will 'short out' the system. The fuse can also be overloaded by an appliance working harder than usual, causing it to want more current than the wiring is rated to, thus blowing the fuse rather than melting the wiring, for example a worn-out bilge-pump motor struggling to pump water out.

Trigger wire

Live battery wire

▲ *Ignition fuse.*

Relay

Solenoid

Starter motor

Starting the engine by connecting the solenoid straight to the battery

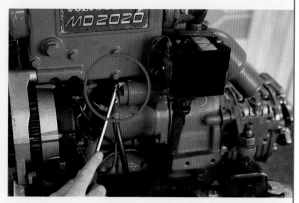

A screwdriver or wire from the trigger wire to the battery wire on the solenoid will activate the starter motor. Ideally make the connection using a wire with suitable connections at each end and a push button switch in the middle - see the video. But in an emergency it can even be done with a screwdriver. This procedure needs to be done with extreme caution.

See the spark? The engine is turning over and starting.

 Scan this QR code to watch a video on how to start a diesel engine by connecting the live and trigger wire to the starter solenoid.

Power consumption by item

Item	Amps	Average hrs used in 24 hrs	Consumption in 24 hrs (amp hours)
Navigation lights	3.7		
Steaming light	1		
Tricolour	1	8	8
Anchor light	1		
Autohelm	5	16	80
Chart plotter	1	24	24
Navigation instruments	0.5	24	12
VHF radio/transmit	1.5		
VHF radio/standby	0.3	24	7.2
Radar transmit	2.5	8	20
Bilge pump	5.0	5 mins	0.4
F/W pump	5.0	5 mins	0.4
Shower pump	8.0	5 mins	0.7
Refrigerator	5.0	12	60
Anchor windlass	150		
Stereo	1.0	2	2
			213.70

You will find fuses in the switch panel and under the companionway for general area type switches.

This is a list of everything you might expect to find on a sailing boat of under 20 metres in length, the current they draw, the typical usage and thus the drain on the domestic battery over 24 hours. The domestic deep-cycle battery will need to be recharged during the 24 hours by running the engine.

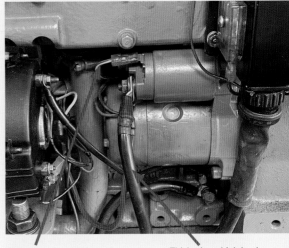

Thin wire – low load   Thick wire – high load

Looking after the electrics

They don't do very much and so all we need to do is to make sure all electrical connections are clean, dry and corrosion-free, and that connections are firm, not loose. If a connection is loose, this will result in an intermittent contact, which can generate heat. If this is a starter motor connection where a high current is passing through, the connection will get hot and could damage the wires. It could ultimately catch fire.

◆ HT leads

A diesel engine is quite resilient when it comes to damp and wet and operates quite happily in this environment. It is only when components corrode that trouble occurs. Petrol engines, however, are different, because they have spark plugs, which require an extremely high voltage, usually over 20,000 volts in order to generate a spark. In older engines this spark is produced by an ignition coil. This is sent down a high-tension lead (HT lead – otherwise known as a 'spark plug lead') to a distributor, which is turned by the engine and distributes power down additional HT leads to each spark plug in turn. Damp can play a big part in causing a misfire because it allows the voltage to divert to earth, which reduces the voltage to the spark plug. So the HT leads, distributor and ignition

coil must be kept clean and dry. WD-40 and a cloth will usually do the job.

In more modern petrol engines the HT leads and distributor are replaced by individual ignition coils, which fit directly on to each spark plug and that are controlled by the engine control unit (ECU) to spark at the correct time. As there is now no requirement for HT leads and a distributor, the system is more reliable and less affected by damp.

Common causes of electrical failure

The most common cause is corrosion, on electrical connections where wires meet, especially on batteries. It is important to protect terminals to ensure a clean contact between the terminals and the wires – positive and negative – that are attached to them. Coating in vaseline will stop corrosion from forming on any bare electrical terminals.

◆ Battery maintenance

Look after your batteries and they will last you a long time. So, battery maintenance saves you money.

Many batteries nowadays are sealed and these have indicators on them to let you know whether they are in good condition or not.

THERE ARE FIVE DIFFERENT TYPES OF BATTERY

Flooded batteries: These are wet cell lead-acid batteries that need the electrolyte to be topped up with distilled water on a regular basis.

Sealed batteries: These are also lead acid but they are sealed with an indicator on the side to let you know the condition of the battery. These do not need to be topped up. In fact, there is no access to the cells.

VRLA – Valve-regulated lead-acid batteries: These are also sealed and have a mechanism to allow for the safe release of gases during charging.

AGM – Absorbed glass matt batteries: These are also wet cell batteries and have the electrolyte suspended in close proximity to the plates in the battery, which is supposed to enhance the discharge and recharge efficiency.

Gel batteries: Like the AGM, this battery has the electrolyte suspended close to the plates but here it is in a gel form with a silica additive. A gel battery is ideally suited to deep-cycle domestic use.

▲ This battery has a good charge, nearly 13 volts with no load.

▲ Under load, this battery drops to 11.6 volts. This battery is in good condition.

▲ This battery is not in good shape. It had only just been charged and yet with no load it was only capable of delivering 12 volts.

▲ Under load, it manages only 10.5 volts. Weak, as the indicator tells us. Time to get a new battery.

HOW TO MAKE YOUR OWN DISTILLED WATER

Distilled water is water that has boiled to become steam and then this steam has cooled to become water again. The boiling removes any minerals and salts within the water.

You will need: A large stainless-steel pot and lid, cake stand or similar type of rack, heat resistant (Pyrex) glass bowl, ice, oven gloves, tap water.

▲ *The kit: big bowl with lid, small bowl, frozen peas.*

1. Put the cake stand into the stainless-steel pot.
2. Half fill the pot with water.
3. Place the glass bowl into the pot, floating on the water. The idea of the cake stand is to stop the glass bowl from touching the bottom of the pot.
4. Turn the lid of the pot upside down.
5. Fill the lid of the pot with ice.
6. Bring the water to the boil and allow it to boil for a good 30 minutes. With the oven gloves you can lift off the lid to check that you have not boiled the water dry. You may have to replace the ice as necessary.
7. Remove the lid and you will see water in the glass bowl.

What has happened is that the water has boiled and steam has risen and hit the cold lid of the pot, condensed out as water, run down the lid to the centre of the lid and dripped into the bowl. The water in the bowl is thus distilled water.

▲ *Boil: the water in the big bowl boils, steam rises, hits the cool lid of the big bowl (the frozen peas keep the lid cool) and then condenses out as distilled water, runs to the centre of the lid and drops into the small bowl.*

▲ *The result. Not a lot for 30 minutes boiling really.*

▲ *It took Jonathan less time to go to Halfords and buy 5 litres of the stuff for not a lot of money.*

The electrolyte and plates

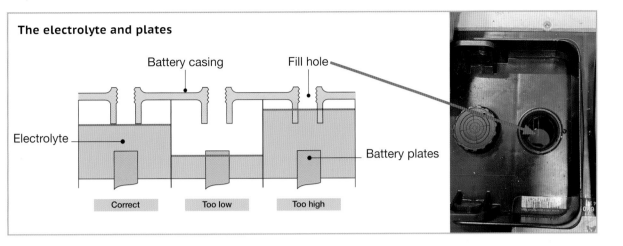

Where you have a battery that's not sealed, this will require the electrolyte inside to be topped up with distilled water every so often. The level of the electrolyte should be just above the plates inside the battery. So, this is something you need to check regularly.

Charging batteries is all part of the maintenance. A battery should hold its charge for about six months.

Note: Batteries will take longer to charge up than the time it took for you to use that amount of charge – but working out how long a battery needs to recharge after discharge is not easy and the example below shows a way you could try to work this out.

The heavy-duty engine start battery, which delivers a large current for a short time, has the charge replaced very quickly by the alternator. Say the time taken to start the engine was 2 seconds and that 200 amps were used by the starter motor, the alternator is able to charge the battery at 30A, then it will take 200A ÷ 30A = 6.7 seconds to replace the 200A that were used.

A lot of factors, however, can make this simple equation unreliable:
- battery condition
- alternator performance
- current lost through connections and wiring
- other electrical use while the engine is running

The main factor is that the alternator rarely puts out the current it is rated to. An alternator will have a maximum rating of perhaps 30 or maybe 120 amps, depending on the type. However, if a battery is fully charged the battery will resist charging and the alternator will sense this and may only charge at a rate of just 2 amps. If starting the battery used 200 amps then replacing it at a rate of 2 amps is going to take a lot longer than the 6.7 seconds of the example above.

One of the biggest problems with batteries on boats is using them infrequently and charging the batteries even more infrequently.

Your boat is on a swinging mooring near the mouth of a river. You start the engine, which depletes the battery by 10 per cent of its charge. You run the engine for about 10 minutes to get out into open water where you can set your sails. The alternator only has a chance to put 5 per cent of the charge back into the battery. The battery now is at 95 per cent charge. When you return you start the engine again and use 10 per cent. Now the battery is at 85.5 per cent charge and you return 4.28 per cent to the battery, having run for ten minutes to get back on to your mooring. If you do that weekend after weekend, you will very quickly find that the engine will sound very sluggish when starting and eventually the battery will have so little charge left in it that it won't be able to start the engine at all.

At this point you need to go to a dock and plug into mains electricity and give your engine battery a good charge. Ideally, if you are on a swinging mooring and you don't have a generator that you can use to charge batteries, or another charging means – solar, wind – you should hook up to the shore at least every six months to charge up your batteries.

Everyone who has a marina berth with electricity will have their boat plugged in and will be trickle charging

CHECKING THE STATE OF YOUR BATTERY

Standard battery indicators do not really tell you the health of your battery. For that you need to test the specific gravity of the electrolyte with a hydrometer, or use a battery load tester available from most motor factors.

Alternatively, charge it up fully, then remove all connections or switch off the battery so there is nothing that could be discharging it. Leave for a few days then take a voltage reading, it should read 12.6V or more. If the reading is below this figure, then it is discharging on its own and should be replaced. A fully charged 12V battery should read 12.6V or above and will not discharge from this for 6 months when there is no load on it.

To save the faff of the above, get a modern battery monitor. They will give you the health of your battery in a few clicks.

▼ *A modern battery monitor.*

constantly. You can't overcharge the battery as the trickle charge only cuts in if the voltage level in the battery dips below a certain level. The battery charger simply keeps an eye on the battery voltage and cuts in when required.

When a wet cell battery is charging, the electrolyte evaporates off, which is why we need to top it up regularly with distilled water.

If you leave a boat with both the heavy-duty engine battery and the deep-cycle domestic battery turned off then there will be nothing discharging the battery and very little need for the battery charger to cut in.

◆ Galvanic action – and the sacrificial anode

A battery is made up of two dissimilar metals that are electrically connected to each other and which are surrounded by an electrolyte – salt water or acid, for example.

So if you have a boat moored in sea water and it has a stainless-steel propeller connected to an aluminium outdrive, you have in effect a giant battery.

And when you have two metals connected to each other in this situation, you get galvanic corrosion where the weaker metal will corrode. It is the same in your battery, which is why the plates corrode, they are made of two dissimilar types of metal.

We have a scale of metals and some metals are more 'noble' than others. In other words, stronger or less likely to react and corrode. So, to protect the weaker metals and prevent them corroding we attach a sacrificial anode, usually made of zinc, to the boat. This is one of the weakest metals of all and will corrode first, thus saving other weak metal on the boat that we are trying to protect.

You will have seen the pear-shaped anodes on hulls and anodes on propeller shafts, or trim tabs. We also have them in the engine. A heat exchanger may have an anode and there can be up to four heat exchangers on a boat. All of them may have raw water flowing through them and they will very likely be made from two different metals. The casing may be made from aluminium and the section where the water flows may well be a bronze alloy because bronze is the best conductor of heat and so a sacrificial anode is required to protect the aluminium, which is the weaker metal. Here, bronze is the stronger metal, then aluminium

Sacrificial anode fitted to an outboard engine

Anode

Corroded

▲ *The brushes here, carbon and spring-loaded so they make contact with the propeller shaft, connect the shaft to the circuit with all the other anodes on the boat to protect the components on the boat – engine, underwater gear – from corrosion.*

and then zinc. The zinc being the weakest of the three will corrode first and the aluminium will be protected.

It is important that each anode is connected to what it is trying to protect – heat exchangers in engines, propellers and shafts, trim tabs. This is especially important when the two differing metals we want to protect are already in contact with each other.

An anode bolted to the bottom of a fibreglass hull above a bronze propeller connected to a stainless-steel shaft mounted on a bronze P-bracket with a bronze rudder aft is a good example of this. Inside the boat will be several electrical cables, usually yellow and green, that connect this anode to the rudder bolts, P-bracket bolts and propeller shaft via spring-mounted carbon brush sets that lean on the shaft as it spins around, completing the circuit to the shaft and the attached propeller, in order that the sacrificial zinc anode erodes before any of the other metal components.

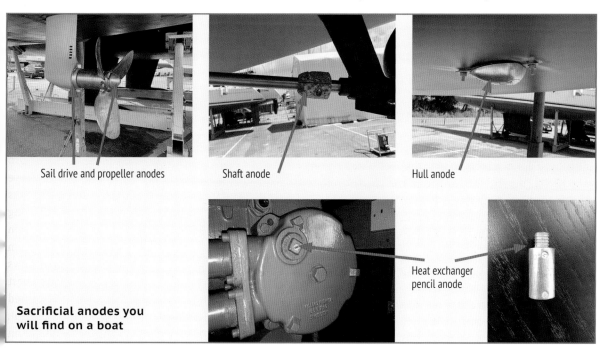

Sail drive and propeller anodes

Shaft anode

Hull anode

Heat exchanger pencil anode

Sacrificial anodes you will find on a boat

◆ Monitoring the alternator when under engine

An alternator is a generator that creates AC current and then converts it into DC and, via a regulator, charges the batteries. The regulator controls the amount of charge required.

And the alternator is run by a belt from the engine. This belt, its condition and the amount of tension form part of the daily engine checks.

▲ *You shouldn't be able to move it more than about 1cm (¼ – ½ inch) of play in total.*

240-volt systems on board

A 240-volt system can be fed from shore power, via a generator or by using an inverter attached to a 12-volt battery.

Battery chargers will be powered by 240-volt shore power. They convert the AC 240 into DC 12 volts and then into a charging voltage to trickle charge the batteries.

When plugged in to shore power, a battery charger also provides the 12-volt power for all your appliances and units. So, when plugged in to 240-volt shore power your 12-volt supply is coming from the charger rather than the domestic battery

It's important to have an idea of the sort of amperage you are using when alongside and that you have a battery charger that is capable of delivering at least this, so that with everything on it has enough amperage available to provide what you require and more to be able to charge the batteries. If you are drawing 20 amps from the kit on the boat and the charger is rated for 5 amps then the other 15 amps will be coming from your domestic

TIP: WINDLASS WARNING

Keep the engine running when raising or lowering the anchor on an electric windlass. The windlass uses a good deal of power and the regulator will be calling for charge from the alternator when you operate the windlass. It will help to give the windlass the power it needs.

TIP: BATTERY OVERHEATING?

Don't immediately blame the charger as 99 times out of 100 it will be the battery that is at fault. Remember, the battery will provide an increasing level of resistance to the battery charger as it becomes more fully charged. A point will be reached when the level of resistance tells the battery charger to stop charging, so if the battery does not provide this resistance the charger will keep charging. The fact that the charger keeps on charging and the battery is overheating indicates that the battery is faulty because it is not providing resistance to the charger to tell it to stop, not the fault of the charger. Therefore, a battery that is overheating is more than likely a sign that the battery is faulty and needs replacing.

battery and the battery charger won't have any amps left over for charging the domestic battery and it will run down and go flat.

You can get battery chargers that are rated at 4, 10, 20, 40, 80 amps, so work out your maximum power requirement by checking the power consumption table (see page 95) and then make sure you have a battery charger that's capable of delivering a bit more than this. Say you require 30 amps with everything on, then get a 40-amp battery charger. It's a bit like an engine, you don't want to go flat out all the time. You want to run at about 80 per cent.

Of course, if your battery charger is a fairly low amperage charger then you will need to turn most things off on your boat for it to be able to charge the battery. Again, check what you are using with the power consumption table.

The amperage of your battery charger will be written on it somewhere. This will be the output in amps.

◆ How a battery charger works

A battery charger will only start charging a battery when it senses a drop in voltage, and when it senses that the battery is at the correct voltage the charger will switch off. This is a safety system, to avoid overcharging.

In fact, as the battery is being charged it provides a resistance to the battery charger, which increases the nearer to being fully charged the battery becomes, and this is what tells the charger when to stop charging.

You might be interested to know that when you switch off the domestic battery you do not actually disconnect everything from the battery. Automatic bilge pumps, for example, are connected directly to the battery, bypassing the battery switch. Some automatic bilge pumps are activated when the level of water in the bilges causes a float switch to float, which switches on the pump until the level of water drops and the float switch turns the pump off. There are some automatic bilge pumps that are not triggered by a switch but which activate themselves at regular intervals regardless of the level of water in the bilges. They turn on and then if there is no load on the pump – no water to pump – they will turn off. This means that regardless of there being any water in the bilge to pump out, they will be using the battery on a regular basis. This is not the type of bilge pump to have if you are on a swinging mooring as it will very quickly run the battery flat. It is all very well to have this type of bilge pump if you are connected to shore power when the boat is in harbour. It would not be my preferred type of bilge pump. I have a bilge pump with a float-switch system.

Apart from automatic bilge pumps, there are other electrical devices that are directly connected to the battery, which use up charge even when the batteries are switched off. Any electrical device that has to memorise anything, such as a stereo that holds your preferred radio stations, will have a permanent feed. You switch the 'Entertainment/HiFi' switch on at the switch panel and you can then turn on the stereo but actually it has been drawing current all the while – just a little – from the battery so it doesn't lose the information stored in it.

Jonathan says

During an investigation on a boat to work out why the domestic battery was being run down when it was supposedly switched off and why the battery charger was cutting in frequently to recharge the battery, I discovered something interesting.

I was aware that the radio with CD player would be wired directly to the battery and using a little current all the time to prevent losing the programme memory. So I turned off the domestic battery and listened to see if I could find the culprit. There was nothing that could have been drawing any current. The automatic bilge pump was not running, the fridge was off, navigation instruments off, VHF and radar off, navigation lights off, interior lights off. Nothing on. The boat was silent. Silent except for a slight whining noise, which seemed to be coming from the CD/radio. Putting my ear to it, it became quite distinct. I pressed eject and the tray came out and the whining noise stopped. I pressed the tray in and not a sound. Somehow, the CD player had become confused and thought that there was a CD in the tray and was spinning and so using a good deal more current than is required to hold the radio station memory and the time.

Turning the batteries off and listening to see if there are any whining or whirring noises will tell you if anything is drawing current and then it is a matter of whether it should be or not. It's worth checking.

Engine instrumentation

When you turn on the ignition you will see an array of warning lights on the engine panel. The number will depend on how sophisticated your engine is but will always include:

- oil pressure
- temperature
- charging

They will also be accompanied by an audible alarm. All warning lights will come on when the ignition is powered up and self-test – just like they do on the dashboard of a car, to show that all the circuits are working. Most will then extinguish but the oil pressure and charging

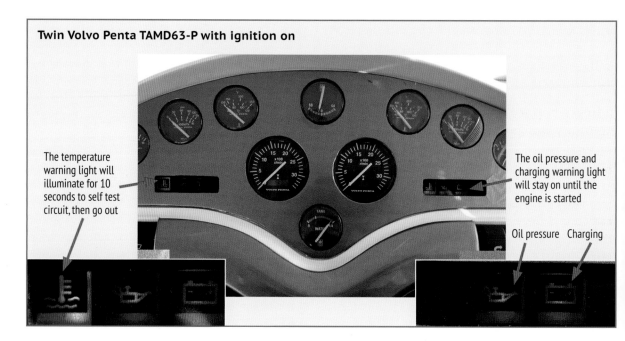

Twin Volvo Penta TAMD63-P with ignition on

The temperature warning light will illuminate for 10 seconds to self test circuit, then go out

The oil pressure and charging warning light will stay on until the engine is started

Oil pressure   Charging

light will stay on. These lights will extinguish once the engine is running, assuming that everything is working properly. So, if you turn on the ignition and any of the lights that should come on don't, you know there is a problem with that circuit.

Let's say the oil pressure light does not come on. You will still hear an alarm sound from the other lights that come on to show that their systems are working. But if you don't notice that the oil light has not come on and you start up regardless, when do you imagine that you might notice some issue with the oil pressure?

When you lose power and a knocking noise starts up and then shortly after the engine seizes. That's when.

You see, lubricating the engine is vital, but once oil pressure is lost it is only the warning light and alarm that alert you to the problem. If there is a problem with that circuit and you don't get the oil light coming on or its alarm, then unless you spot the lack of the light you won't know you have a problem.

So, check that all the lights that should come on at the engine start up, do come on.

A seized engine, after all, is extremely expensive to repair or replace. And all for want of a few litres of oil, more than likely.

So, what about the charging light? It should come on when the ignition is on and the engine is not running. If it doesn't then you know there is an issue with the alternator circuit and it will not charge the battery when the engine is started. Also, if the charging light comes on at any point when the engine is running you know that the alternator is no longer charging the battery, because when all is well that light will go out.

The most common reason for the alternator light coming on is a broken drive belt and if this is ignored then after a few minutes you can expect the overheating light to come on, because in many cases the same belt also drives the engine cooling circulation pump!

Scan this QR code to watch a video on how to change a drive belt.

Jonathan says

We have talked about looking after your batteries, making sure they are topped up, clean, dry and corrosion-free. Well, I am reminded of a fishing boat I was called to off the Needles in Alum Bay, Isle of Wight. He reported an explosion that had occurred under the floor of the boat after trying to start the engine. Not sure what to do next, he called for help.

I found the boat was intact and having established there was no fire, we lifted the lazarette where the noise had come from. There was a battery loosely fitted to the rear of the space and it was clearly the cause of the explosion as there was a hole in the top of the battery and battery acid had sprayed everywhere!

The battery was over 8 years old, had never been topped up with distilled water and the terminals were very corroded, as a result of the damp environment.

After removal of the old battery, a good clean-up of the terminals on the wires and adding a new battery, we got him up and running again.

But what caused the old battery to explode? Well, neglect basically.

1. Not checking the fluid levels will eventually, through natural gassing, cause the tops of the plates and importantly the plate connectors to become exposed inside the battery housing.
2. A damp atmosphere causing the exposed plate connectors to corrode.
3. Being at anchor using battery power causes gassing from the battery. This gassing would have been much greater than normal because of the low level of the electrolyte in the battery – the battery had never been topped up with distilled water – which meant the battery had to work harder to hold its charge.
4. The fact that the battery was not secured in the boat, which resulted in excessive movement and jolting, which broke the already corroded internal plate connections.
5. Finally, starting the engine, which created a spark between the now corroded and broken internal plate connectors, igniting the highly explosive hydrogen gas. Being in a confined battery box caused the battery to expand rapidly and as the casing broke under pressure, so the battery exploded.

So please look after your batteries.
- Failing to carry out simple preventative measures could cause a devastating accident. Imagine if the battery in the case of the call-out had made a hole in the hull of the boat.
- Remember, battery acid is highly corrosive and will burn your skin immediately on contact.
- Always store your batteries in a ventilated box, which if the worst happened would help contain the acid within it.

A battery that is gassing excessively will be hot and will smell of sulphur – the same smell you get from anaerobic water in the lavatory in the heads. So, if you smell sulphur, check that it is not coming from the battery compartment. Batteries normally gas at their worst when being charged so if you smell sulphur, turn off the battery charger and isolate the batteries using the battery switches. This will allow the batteries to cool and they can then be replaced. NEVER get close to a battery when it is gassing as it could explode!

The result of overcharging a battery – perhaps a damaged battery where a cell has broken down so that the battery does not send the correct resistance back to the charger to tell it to stop charging, or very rarely a faulty battery charger – is that you get excessive gassing. A little gassing occurs normally during regular charging but when a lead-acid battery is overcharged, the electrolyte solution can overheat and this creates hydrogen and oxygen gases, which increases the pressure inside the battery.

A standard unsealed, lead-acid battery has the capacity to vent the excess hydrogen and oxygen and to recirculate these gases to the battery.

If the amount of gas created is greater than the venting capacity of the battery or there is a malfunction in the venting system, the electrolyte solution in the battery can be boiled out of the battery. If the electrolyte solution falls below the level required to reach the charge plates, the exposed charge plates will be damaged.

Finally, as happened in the instance above, where the lead-acid battery was overcharging and overheating and creating more hydrogen and oxygen gases than could be vented, the pressure inside the battery overcame it and it exploded.

9 How to look after your engine

Servicing your engine, keeping it clean, staying on top of any issues and looking after it mechanically are just part of the deal. How you treat your engine is just as important, and there are three key things that you should be aware of in terms of care for your engine to get the maximum performance and life out of it.

1. Optimum temperature

All engines have an optimum operating temperature when they will be running at their most efficient and most economic. So, when starting an engine from cold

you need to get to this optimum temperature as quickly as possible without putting the engine under strain.

As we have said, you might think that running an engine on tickover for 5 to 10 minutes from cold is enough to get it warmed up, but it isn't.

To get it warmed up you need to run it for 25 to 30 minutes under some load. So, having made sure that the boat is securely tied to the dock, click her into gear. Turning the propeller will put a load on the engine and encourage more fuelling in the engine and that will then create more combustion, which will create more heat and so the engine will heat up more quickly. If you ran

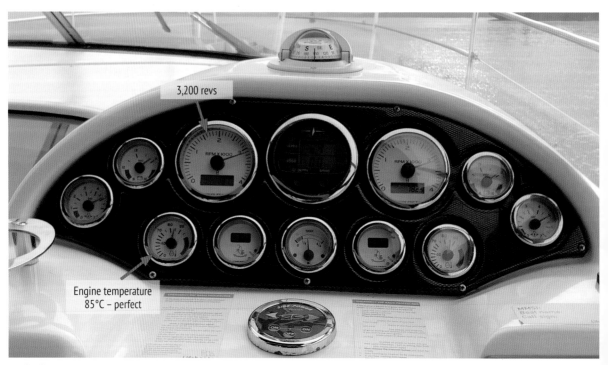

3,200 revs

Engine temperature
85°C – perfect

▲ *Perfect running temperature.*

the engine out of gear in tickover it could take an hour to warm up and even then it would not reach its optimum operating temperature.

You could start the engine, drop the lines and take the boat for a run, being careful not to accelerate too fast. The idea is that by having load on the engine it gets hotter quicker without being put under strain while it is cold by over-revving and straining the engine.

2. Optimum fuelling

Accelerate gently.

Don't run the engine for long periods at full power.

When it comes to fuel consumption, it's worth understanding exactly what's going on. There are plenty of people who run their engines at two speeds – flat out or stopped. Doing this is a sure-fire way of wearing your engine out. Take Formula One, that's what they do and they have to change their engines every few races – actually, as the current rules allow them to use only three engines every season without incurring penalties, they change them roughly every seven races. Still, always running at full throttle is an expensive way to go.

When accelerating, do it gently and progressively. This will put less strain through the rubber bushes, which connect the engine to the gearbox, or the rubber propeller bushes if fitted (sometimes in the place of shear pins on outboards), or the engine itself by overloading it. So always accelerate gently and don't go into full throttle for long periods. Engines are designed to run at about 85 per cent of full throttle and not 100 per cent all the time. So accelerate up to full throttle and then back the throttle off to 85 per cent and that way the engine will run comfortably all day long.

You see, when an engine is running at full throttle it is trying to over-power itself, over-fuelling, trying to go faster than it physically can go. It is feeding more fuel into the cylinders than it can handle in order to try and get the most power it can deliver and this is not only a waste of fuel, it also wears the engine out. Full throttle means that the engine is trying to go faster than full throttle and this creates more load on the engine, which generates more heat and wears things out more quickly.

In fact, backing off the throttle to 85 per cent will actually only lose you between 5 and 10 per cent of boat speed. It has to do with the Law of Diminishing Returns.

Propeller bushes are either rubber or bronze and designed to fail through impact or overloading to protect the gearbox from damage.

Propeller bush is pressed into the prop body

▲ *Rubber bush on a propeller designed to break if the propeller gets caught and thus protect the gearbox from damage.*

Slot where shear pin fits into propeller

Shear pin

▲ *Shear pin designed to break if the propeller gets caught and thus protect the gearbox from damage (Mercury 3.3hp outboard).*

Fuel economy versus speed

This is all very approximate but it gives you an idea of the saving.

Boat	Speed at 100% throttle	Fuel consumption at 100% throttle	Cost at £1.20/l per hour	Speed at 85% throttle 10% off full speed	Fuel consumption at 85% throttle 33% less than full speed	Cost at £1.20/l per hour
Princess 23M twin diesel	35 knots	454lph	£545	32 knots	303lph	£364
Nimbus 27 single diesel	35 knots	57lph	£68	32 knots	38lph	£46
8m RIB twin petrol outboard	40 knots	75lph	£90	36 knots	50lph	£60

Also, the amount of fuel you save from 100 per cent to 85 per cent is roughly 30–40 per cent. So, if your boat does 35 knots flat out, backing off to 85 per cent throttle can save you around a third the amount of fuel you were using at 100 per cent and the boat will still be going at about 32 knots through the water. Reducing your boat speed by 20 per cent can save you as much as 50 per cent fuel compared to running flat out.

In some of the modern electronically controlled engines the throttle and fuel feed is matched to the engine revs so the engine is fuelled to make it achieve maximum revs but does not over-fuel it beyond that. These engines have a number of sensors in the engine measuring load, revs, temperatures and so forth and these can control the fuelling a lot better. Older engines don't have these sensors. You can see the effect of 'load' by revving the engine in neutral. It will rev much higher than when you are in gear driving through the water. The difference in the level of revs is the load that the engine is under. The engine is still trying to achieve the same revs as it would have done in neutral. This load is what wears the engine out and so giving the engine every chance to run at its optimal performance level by having it serviced, correctly lubricated, correctly cooled, with sufficient air, clean propellers and a clean hull, will make it last longer.

3. Cooling the engine down

Just as important as warming up is cooling down. Before you turn the engine off after your trip, let it idle for some minutes. This is particularly important if you have just been running the engine hard. The point is that your engine, after running at higher loads, will be hot and it needs to cool down before you turn it off. While the engine is running, cooling raw water is passing through the heat exchanger and is cooling the sealed fresh-water/coolant mixture, which in turn is cooling the engine. So, leaving the engine in tickover for a few minutes will allow the engine to cool itself.

If you turn the engine off as soon as you have moored, this stops the flow of raw water and the fresh-water/coolant mix surrounding the engine will now become superheated by the very hot cylinders. As it heats up so it will expand, increasing the pressure in the sealed system until it escapes as steam through the pressure cap in the header tank. Now you have steam and searing hot antifreeze being sprayed throughout the engine room.

The risk of the engine overheating isn't the only reason we need to be careful when we slow the engine down after high speed. The other reason is to allow any turbo to cool down. Turbos create air pressure and they spin at very high speeds, up to 80,000rpm for marine engines, more in a lot of high-performance cars.

Anything that spins that fast requires efficient lubrication so the turbine and the compressor will be lubricated by oil pumped under pressure, provided by the engine. The minute you turn off the engine, the lubricating oil for the turbo stops being pumped, and if you have something spinning at 80,000rpm it will take some time to slow down to zero. During this time and with no lubrication, the shaft will burn up whatever oil had been there before the engine stopped. It will become hot and could seize. You would certainly be adding excess wear to it at the very least and that could spell problems in the future.

So again, by bringing the engine down to idle for a few minutes means the turbo has a chance to slow right down and then when we turn the engine off it will stop quite quickly.

10 Checks, servicing and winterisation

Checklists are very important. After all, an airline pilot would never board the aeroplane, start up then just take off. No, he or she will go through a strict list of checks that have to be carried out with a co-pilot beforehand. And the same applies for boats: you should not simply get on board and set off without going through your own checklist.

You need to start thinking about your boat in terms of 'What do I need to look out for before I set sail? Which bit if it failed could put me and the boat in danger?' Some people take this to the extreme and it is called 'catastrophising'. This makes sense for Vendée Globe racers and those who go on expeditions but is probably a bit over the top for the average leisure sailor. Nonetheless, it is worth remembering the 'First Rule of Good Seamanship'. That is: 'Try and avoid situations that require good seamanship'. Being prepared is part of good seamanship.

So you should get into a routine of carrying out regular checks and having lists of checks written down to ensure nothing is overlooked. Take a leaf out of the pilots' book. They walk the plane before a flight. You need to walk the boat, from stem to stern, checking everything.

Jonathan says: I would estimate that for about 50 per cent of people in any marina you could drop their anchor into the water and they wouldn't even notice until they attempted to drive off, when of course they would suddenly stop. It's the sort of thing you don't really look for – you may do your engine checks etc, but there is more to it than that. That's why it's a good idea always to 'walk the boat' before boarding and again when on deck.'

Everyday checks and checklists

◆ Cleanliness is next to godliness

Keep the engine bay and bilges clean and dry so it's easy to spot if something starts leaking or something appears in the bilge like a stray nut or a bolt that shouldn't be there. If you don't do regular checks and you don't keep the engine bay clean and dry then you won't notice if something suddenly falls off the engine or you spring a leak, so it is important that you do this. Regular all-round visual checks of the engine noting any deterioration are advisable.

We have said in previous chapters that corrosion is one of the biggest enemies on a boat. The salty, wet atmosphere is perfect for promoting corrosion. It is one of the biggest causes of electrical problems, and of course this atmosphere corrodes metal parts on engines, with the result that things can fall off. So a good visual inspection of the engine, noting any corrosion, is essential.

Look at the engine manufacturer's manual to keep on top of service intervals and what needs to be done at each service. Some of this you will be able to do yourself. Keeping the servicing up to date will give you confidence that components aren't going to clog or fail and your engine will remain trouble-free between services.

◆ Why does the service engineer paint the engine?

Duncan says: I always used to be very impressed with the service I got from engineers in the past. Not only had they serviced the engine but they had also gone to the trouble of painting it a nice smart green colour – it is a Volvo Penta engine.

Jonathan has told me that this has nothing to do with trying to make the job look smart, well not entirely. It does make the job look smart, of course, but there are good reasons for painting the engine. The paint is a corrosion inhibitor. It is usually an aerosol so you need to make sure that it is suitable for spraying electrical components with: some aerosols are, some aren't. Sprayed on to the engine, this 'paint' stops any damp from sitting on components, which might cause surface corrosion, which in turn might lead to that component failing and therefore a breakdown.

Comparing your engine to a car, if you leave your car out overnight in the rain you will find in the morning that the brake disks have rusted. That's what's happening to a marine engine with any damp on it. This is why marine engines are painted, to stop corrosion, so touching up this paint regularly is a good idea.

Some marine engineers don't bother to paint engines they work on. They will change an impeller – unscrew the nuts on the impeller plate, scratch them and the plate, replace the impeller and the gasket and secure the plate and leave it. In a couple of months the plate and the nuts will show surface corrosion. Had the plate and nuts been sprayed they would have remained corrosion-free for at least a year.

And the anti-corrosion paints are colour coded by make of engine:

- Green for Volvo Penta
- Sand coloured for Caterpillar
- Grey for Yanmar
- Red for Beta and Bukh
- White for MAN
- Blue for Thornycroft

Grey – Yanmar; Yamaha

Green – Volvo diesel

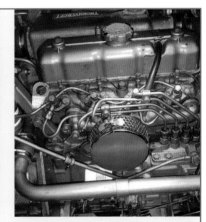

Blue – Thorncroft; Nanni; Perkins

Examples of different engine colours. Some engines are the same colour but they will be different tones. Painting an engine does not just help identify the manufacturer but mainly acts as a barrier to corrosion.

Red – Bukh; Beta; Volvo petrol

Black – Mercury/Mercruiser; Suzuki

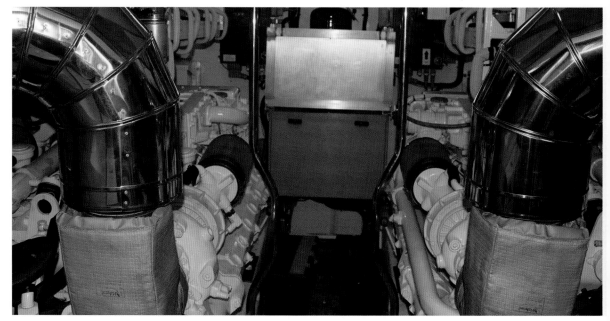
▲ *A pair of MAN engines (white) on a superyacht.*

However, you must try to avoid spraying any rubber parts, such as drive belts, when using the corrosion inhibitor because if sprayed with anything they could slip when you start the engine. If you do accidently spray anything rubber, immediately wipe it off to thin the spray out because a thick coating could penetrate the rubber. Preferably wipe all the paint off the rubber, although you need to be quick as corrosion-inhibiting sprays dry very quickly.

◆ Use your boat

Interestingly, although perhaps not surprisingly, the more you use your boat the better it is for it. Frequent use actually helps prevent breakdowns, because everything is kept from getting too damp and as a result you create less corrosion. There is also a greater chance that you will stay on top of the necessary checks.

Boats on swinging moorings, for example, tend not to be in as good condition as boats moored in marinas because they get visited less often. This sounds like a sweeping generalisation and some boats on swinging moorings will be used regularly and well cared for. But looking back over ten years of breakdown call-outs, the swinging moorings theory holds true. Worth considering when it comes to buying a boat – where has it been kept or moored?

◆ Checking drive belts

Checking the drive belts means checking the tension and wear.
- Tension – press down in the centre of the longest part of the belt and you shouldn't be able to move it more than 0.5cm (¼ inch) – 1 cm (½ inch) of play in total. On the newer type of flat belt you also shouldn't be able to twist the belt more than 90 degrees.
- Wear – excessive black dust around the belt tells you it is wearing out and it is likely to start slipping. It needs to be changed. You will see black dust gather due to normal belt wear, so wipe it away rather than letting it build up and keep an eye on it. That way you can see instantly if it is creating more black dust than is normal, which tells you the belt needs to be changed.

◆ Battery checks

Wet cell batteries may have a condition indicator known as a 'magic eye'. This is fitted to the top of the battery and is a circular lens that changes colour depending on the battery's state of charge and condition.
- No indicators - you need to remove the plastic caps and check that the electrolyte is covering the plates. If not, top up with distilled water to the correct level as shown on the side of every battery.

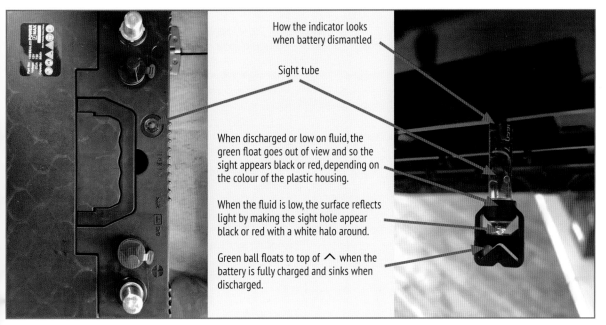

How the indicator looks when battery dismantled

Sight tube

When discharged or low on fluid, the green float goes out of view and so the sight appears black or red, depending on the colour of the plastic housing.

When the fluid is low, the surface reflects light by making the sight hole appear black or red with a white halo around.

Green ball floats to top of ∧ when the battery is fully charged and sinks when discharged.

▲ *Battery condition indicator.*

- Green indicator – fully charged and level OK.
- Black or red indicator – indicating discharged.
- Black or red indicator with a white circle – electrolyte level low, requiring topping up.

Most batteries with indicators should have a description on them as to what each colour represents.

◆ Engine checklists

Have a look at the engine checklists below. Remember, the checks don't end once you have finished your journey. It is always best practice to check over your engine once again at the end of your trip to spot any issues that require resolving in plenty of time for your next departure.

Daily – before starting
- Check sufficient fuel in tank.
- Check battery switch ON.
- Check engine oil level.
- Check belt tension.
- Check raw-water strainer.
- Check engine sea cock is open.
- Check bilge for leakage of oil, fuel, water.

Start engine – after starting
- Check cooling water flow (exhaust).
- Check engine oil pressure (instrument panel – oil pressure gauge).
- Check battery charging (instrument panel – voltmeter/ammeter).
- Check no rope is hanging overboard.

After sailing
- Allow engine to idle for some minutes.
- Stop engine.
- Switch off unnecessary electrical equipment (or switch off engine battery isolator).
- Shut engine sea cock.

Secrets to reliability
- Keep engine bay and bilges clean and dry.
- Regular all-round visual check of the engine noting any deterioration.
- Service as per manufacturer's instructions.
- Coat engine with corrosion inhibitor regularly.
- Use the boat as much as possible.
- If you run the engine while alongside for any period, put it in gear.
- Keep fuel tank as full as practical, never go below half.

- Inspect fuel pre-filter regularly (monthly, depending on use). Remove elements.
- Check seals on fuel filler caps.
- Check for belt dust and signs of wear.
- Use a fuel additive to prevent bug.
- Check battery water levels regularly.

Servicing

There is a saying in the commercial marine world:

'Carrying out maintenance is expensive …

… Not carrying out maintenance is even more expensive.'

◆ The importance of servicing

It goes without saying that looking after things means they will serve you well and last longer.

The minimum annual service your engine should receive is:

Fuel system

- Primary fuel filter/water separator – clean the glass/see-through bowl and change the filter.
- Change the secondary fuel filter.

You will have introduced air into the fuel system and so a diesel engine will need to be bled.

Oil system

- Change the engine oil and oil filter.
- Change the gearbox oil and filter (if filter fitted).

Cooling system

- Fresh-water system – check the coolant (the fresh-water/antifreeze mix) level and strength with a coolant tester, which we will talk about a bit later in this chapter.
- Raw-water system – check and clean the strainer, replace the impeller in the raw-water pump.

Engine anodes

Check anodes that may be fitted to the engine, heat exchanger, intercooler, gearbox cooler and/or oil coolers. Replace if more than 25 per cent corroded (you will need to compare it to a new one to tell how much it is corroded).

Air system

- Change the air filter

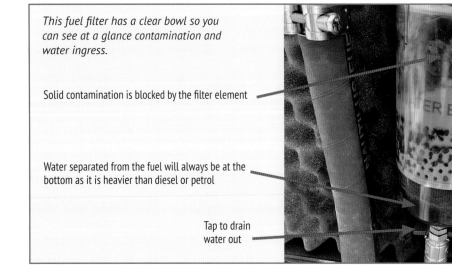

This fuel filter has a clear bowl so you can see at a glance contamination and water ingress.

Solid contamination is blocked by the filter element

Water separated from the fuel will always be at the bottom as it is heavier than diesel or petrol

Tap to drain water out

Electrical system

- Check the battery voltage.
- Top up with distilled water if it is a wet battery.
- Check terminals.
- Alternator drive belt – check for wear, replace if necessary.

◆ Mechanical moving parts

- Control cables – throttle cable, gear cable, stop cable and levers. Check that all cables are lubricated, greased, not seizing up or stiff and free from corrosion.

When a control cable starts to get stiffer, it is an indication that it is time to replace it. The cable is struggling to move within the sleeve it travels in, the metal is becoming fatigued and will end up breaking. Stiffness creeps up on you and the skipper often doesn't notice the stiffness in a throttle cable or gear lever. It is only when someone who is not familiar with the boat operates the levers that they will comment, 'Goodness, this is stiff'.

No one ever sets a service interval for a control cable. They are fairly inexpensive, fairly easy to change and fairly catastrophic when they fail. It is worth scheduling a change of control cables every five years.

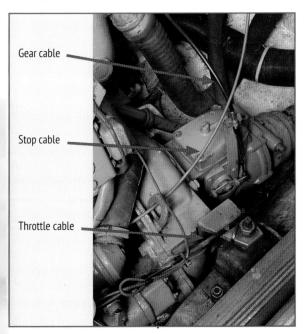

Gear cable

Stop cable

Throttle cable

▲ *Some people even have the spare cable in place ready to swap over if needed.*

Duncan says: My gear cable snapped just as I was going into reverse gear to take way off the boat as I entered my finger berth, ready for a single-handed return to the dock. I wasn't going that fast, of course, and was able to get my stern bridle on to the cleat on the dock and surge the way off the boat. Not the single-handed technique I recommend. We always take all way off the boat before lassoing a cleat on shore, except in an emergency like that, when we can't.

- Steering cables – check and grease these, too.
- Winches – service.
- Sea cocks – check their movement and condition and grease.
- Generators are diesel or petrol engines that generate voltage rather than turn a shaft for propulsion, and so they require exactly the same daily checks as engines – oil, coolant levels, raw-water strainer, drive belt and checks for leaks. In terms of servicing, they require the same attention as an engine.
- *Additionally, check the engine bay fire extinguishers.* Fire extinguishers generally require annual maintenance, check the manufacturer's recommendations.

GENERATOR TIP

Always run a diesel generator with at least 50 per cent of its rated load. Never run it for long periods with a light load. A light load will mean the engine is not having to work hard, it will not reach its optimum working temperature. The temperature in the cylinders will not be high enough to burn the fuel completely and this will build up sooty deposits. You will know when the generator does not have enough load on it because there will be black smoke coming out of its exhaust. So if you are downwind of a boat that is running a generator and there is black smoke coming out of it, ask them to turn a few more things on: a radiator, the oven, hob, heating, air conditioning, to increase the load and the black smoke will disappear.

CHECK THE FILTERS ON ANY FRESH-WATER DOMESTIC PUMP

Water can leave deposits over time and filters on fresh-water domestic pumps can become blocked. Make sure you know where the fresh-water domestic pump is and how to remove the filter, clean it and replace it. Check the manual for the pump. Signs that the filter is blocking up could be a reduced water flow at the tap.

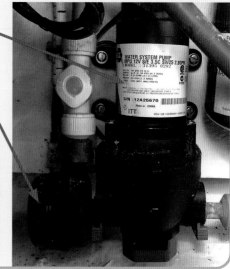

Domestic fresh-water pump

A filter is fitted into the input side of the pump to protect it from contamination

Clear filter cover

Filter

Beyond this, in terms of servicing you need to keep an eye on:

Below decks

- the bilges – clean bilges are kind to the bilge pump; dirty bilges will simply block up an automatic pump, seize it up and result in it being replaced
- the gas system
- any air-conditioning system
- any central heating, air or diesel
- heads, manual or electric
- shower and water pumps
- fridges and freezers
- any electric device, be it a door or sliding window
- sea cocks
- alarms

On deck

- the electric pasarelle
- the submersible bathing platform
- davits, manual and electric
- cranes
- winches, manual and electric
- windlasses, manual and electric
- standing rigging – corrosion
- running rigging – chafe

The hull

When out of the water:

- Check the number of skin fittings = the number of sea cocks.
- Check the condition of the propeller shaft and propellers.
- Check the condition of trim tabs and stern gear – rudders.
- Replace hull anodes and propeller/trim tab anodes.

Winterising your boat

Winterising is the business of shutting all the systems down on the boat and preparing them and protecting them for the duration of the winter months ready for re-commissioning in the spring. The degree to which you have to winterise a boat that is to be left unattended through the winter depends on whether you are leaving it in the water or on the hard, where the boat is and the severity of the weather.

If you expect really low temperatures then you need to take care that pipes that carry water are either empty in case they might freeze over and burst, or that there is plenty of antifreeze in the pipes along with the water.

So, here is a list of everything you need to do and you can take out of it what you need, depending on where your boat is.

Remember, winterising isn't just about the engines, it is about protecting the whole boat.

◆ What are you winterising?

- fuel tanks
- engines: inboard engines (petrol and diesel), gearboxes, shafts, propellers, sterndrives and outboards (petrol and diesel)
- water tanks: pressurised and non-pressurised domestic water system, grey water system and black water/holding tank
- batteries: heavy-duty and domestic
- the boat: internally, the fittings and furnishings; externally, its integrity

◆ Fuel tanks

You could use an endoscope to see the state of the tank and book a tank clean-out. (Have I ever done this? Er no. But Jonathan does, regularly.)

Or, simply:

- Diesel – top the tank up full and add an anti-diesel-bug solution.
- Petrol – top the tank up to 95 per cent to allow for expansion and add a system-cleaning solution.

◆ Inboard petrol or diesel engines

Fuel system

Fuel filters. If you are not going to use the boat for any length of time then you should change the fuel filters. Any dirt or water in the filters makes for perfect conditions for growing the diesel-bug bacteria and diesel bug will grow in the fuel filters over the winter. So, if you change the filters and you have nice clean fuel with an anti-diesel bug additive, there is no chance of that happening. If you have a petrol engine then a fuel additive is a good idea, not a performance-enhancing additive but a system-cleaning additive to remove the build-up of deposits and keep the fuel system in the engine clean.

Oil system

The same can be said for the oil system. You don't want to be leaving dirty oil in the engine during the winter, so you should change the engine oil and the oil filters.

Check the gearbox oil

At the back of the engine you will find the gearbox. This is attached via a coupling to the propeller shaft, which goes out of the back of the boat via the stern seal. And assuming your boat is staying in the water for the winter you need to make sure that the stern seal is not leaking. If there are any drips from it you need to adjust it or replace it. Of course, if your stern gland is the stuffing box type then a drip every 20 seconds is about right while running but should only drip occasionally if at all when stationary. Anything more than this needs to be investigated.

◆ Cooling system

Direct cooling – this is where raw water passes round the outside of the engine to cool it.

Indirect cooling/Closed loop system – this is where you have a two-stage cooling system where raw water passes through a heat exchanger, which cools a fresh-water/antifreeze mix (coolant). Raw water also passes through intercoolers (for the turbo or supercharger) and oil coolers.

Raw-water system

Cleaning the raw-water system is important to remove any build-up of salts or minerals. If you leave raw water in the system over the winter period, a build-up of lime scale and salts can form and this will start to affect the cooling system's capacity and so the transfer of heat will be greatly reduced – furring of the pipes, if you like, reduces the diameter and the degree to which the cool temperature of the sea water can be transferred to cool down the hot fresh-water and antifreeze mix that is in the other side of the cooling system.

You should flush the raw-water system with fresh water and then add coolant – a water and antifreeze 50/50 mix. We recommend using a propylene glycol, environmentally friendly antifreeze.

The way you do this depends on two things:

1. Is the raw-water strainer above the water level in the boat?
2. Is the raw-water strainer below the water level in the boat?

In both cases we get the sea-water pump to do the work.

Flushing out the raw water system

Flow to impeller   Water strainer   Hose to keep a constant supply of water while flushing

Pour coolant into the system until it starts to appear at the exhaust. You may need up to 10 litres depending on engine size so have another open and ready just in case.

Raw-water strainer above the waterline

1. Take the lid off the raw-water filter.
2. For engines above 75hp, insert a hose pipe into the raw-water filter and turn on. If your engine is under 75hp you should be able to keep pace with the water consumption by pouring it into the filter from a watering can.
3. Start the engine.
4. Shut off the raw-water sea cock.
5. Run the engine for five minutes, controlling the water flow.
6. Turn off the engine and hose.
7. Start the engine and add coolant to the raw-water filter until seen at the exhaust.
8. Turn off the engine.
9. Check that the raw-water strainer is clean.
10. Replace the strainer and the raw-water filter lid.
11. Open the raw-water sea cock. With the lid on the strainer, the system is sealed and no raw water can enter.

Raw-water strainer below the waterline

1. Turn off the raw-water sea cock.
2. Remove the pipe from the outlet side of the filter.
3. Put the pipe into a bucket of water.
4. Start the engine.

▲ *Pouring water into the raw-water filter on a small engine from a watering can.*

5. Keep the bucket of water topped up by running a hose into it.
6. Turn off the engine.
7. Add coolant to the bucket.
8. Start the engine and run until you see coolant coming out of the exhaust.
9. Turn off the engine.
10. Reattach the pipe to the outlet side of the filter.
11. Replace the lid on the filter.
12. Open the raw-water sea cock. With the lid on the filter, the system is sealed and no raw water can enter.

▲ The Volvo MD 2020.

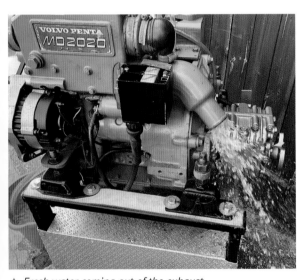

▲ Fresh water coming out of the exhaust.

▲ Pipe from impeller to raw-water sea cock removed (sea cock closed!); pipe/hose from impeller to bucket of water attached.

▲ Now flushing the system with coolant.

  Scan this QR code to watch a video on flushing the raw-water system on a yacht engine and a motorboat engine.

There are some engines, the Volvo KAD and the Yamaha diesel for example, where the raw-water filter is fitted after the impeller, the idea being that if the impeller were to break up, the bits would be caught by the filter. In this case, follow the steps for below the waterline, but instead of removing the pipe from the outlet of the raw-water filter you need to remove the pipe from the inlet of the impeller and fit a pipe to this that you place in a bucket of water.

The pictures above show an example of this.

Raw-water impeller

Next on the raw-water side is to consider the impeller in the raw-water pump. If you are going to change it before recommissioning the engine then you might as well leave it where it is. If you are not going to change it then remove it now to allow the vanes to regain their shape.

Impellers don't like to be left in a fixed state for a long period of time, without being operational and having water passing through them. In fact, if you do leave an impeller in place over the winter it can operate rather poorly, with a reduced flow, when started in the spring. It is always best to start the new season with a new impeller.

Indirect cooling or closed loop cooling

Here, the cooling system uses a fresh-water and anti-freeze mix, referred to as coolant, which passes through a heat exchanger, which is cooled by raw water. So, you need to check the concentration and the condition of the coolant.

The coolant concentration can be tested with either a testing kit or a testing instrument.

Take the cap off the cooling system, put the tube in and suck up some coolant and the number of disks floating will give you the concentration and show you how cold the coolant can get before it would freeze.

The age of the antifreeze is important too. Antifreeze contains corrosion inhibitors and these wear off over time. If the coolant is looking brown – a sign that rust is forming in the engine – then you need to change it and put in some fresh.

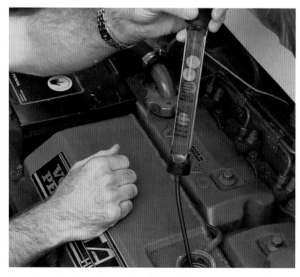

▲ *Discs showing the coolant is good for temperatures down to -34°F or -37°C.*

 Scan this QR code to watch a video on checking the coolant.

COOLANT

Coolant is the term for a fresh-water and antifreeze mix.

- This should be mixed 50/50.
- It is available as a concentrate that you mix or pre-mixed. Do check this and don't dilute a pre-mixed solution.
- Antifreeze has anti-corrosion additives and these generally wear out after 2 years. So, replace the antifreeze/fresh-water mix every 2 years. Antifreeze itself lasts longer than 2 years, it is the anti-corrosion properties that become less effective over time.
- Make sure the antifreeze is propylene glycol based and not ethylene glycol based, which is harmful to the environment. Propylene glycol based antifreeze can be used in drinking-water systems.
- Some antifreezes are designated as 'long life' and can last up to 5 years between changes. The colour of antifreeze may indicate if your antifreeze is 'long life' or not. If it is pink or yellow, this is likely to indicate a long-life antifreeze, so when topping it up you must add the same type of antifreeze, because mixing normal antifreeze with 'long life' antifreeze can cause all the antifreeze to congeal and block the water ways. Simply adding antifreeze of the same colour that is already in there is usually the best course of action.

Duncan says: Don't do what I used to do with the closed-loop fresh-water system on my Volvo Penta MD21B engine. I used to check the level on the header tank rigorously and then top it up regularly with fresh water. I don't know where the water was going but it always needed just a little top-up to the mark. But of course, I was not adding any antifreeze, simply fresh water. So, what had been coolant, a 50/50 mix of fresh water and antifreeze, was becoming over the season simply fresh water – and just in time for winter. Nowadays I add coolant, which I keep handy for top-ups – making sure I buy the environmentally friendly propylene glycol and not the ethylene glycol.

◆ Sterndrives

A sterndrive is powered by an inboard engine. So, winterising the inboard engine follows the steps taken above with the exception that the raw-water intake is on the sterndrive leg itself. There are inlets on the sides of the leg, where you can fit bellows, also referred to as 'ear muffs', 'flush muffs', 'flushers' and a hose with fresh water. The boat needs to be out of the water for this, with the sterndrive in the down position.

Fit the correct bellows for the make of engine. Run the engine, run the water and this will come out of the raw-water outlet by the top of the leg and also through the centre of the propeller, along with the exhaust gases. Run it for 5 to 10 minutes to flush the salt water out.

Sterndrive engines can be difficult to flush with antifreeze because of their design. You cannot simply suck it into the engine via the bellows using the raw-water pump in the engine, because unless the whole sterndrive is underwater, the system is incapable of sucking anything in. When you flushed the system with fresh water, the hose was pushing the water into the system under pressure. So, to get some pressure, place the antifreeze well above the bellows inlet.

Check with the engine manufacturer to see how they advise you should get antifreeze into the raw-water system.

In many cases, once the engine has been flushed with fresh water the whole system is then drained and then left empty for the winterising period. Drains are fitted for this purpose. In the case of raw-water-cooled engines they are fitted to the engine block, exhaust manifolds and circulation pump. In the case of indirectly cooled engines the engine is already protected with coolant so it is only the heat exchangers that need draining.

If you can't get coolant into the raw-water system for the winter, drain all the water out because you don't want to leave any water in the system over the winter as it might freeze. Remember, fresh water will freeze at a higher temperature than salt water and will expand when frozen. Frozen water that expands can cause the pipework to crack.

There is no need to add antifreeze to the raw-water system or to drain it if winter conditions will not be cold.

Some sterndrives have a flushing port. So, instead of using the bellows to flush the sea-water system, attach a hose to the flushing port and flush the system with this. And you can add antifreeze to the raw-water system at this point too.

It is always worth getting some expert advice from someone who knows your particular engine and has experience of flushing the raw water through the system.

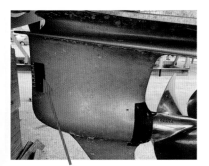

Raw-water intake

 Scan this QR code to watch a video on flushing a raw-water system on an outboard with bellows.

▲ *Bellows fitted to a sterndrive and flushing fresh water through the raw-water cooling system to prevent corrosion.*

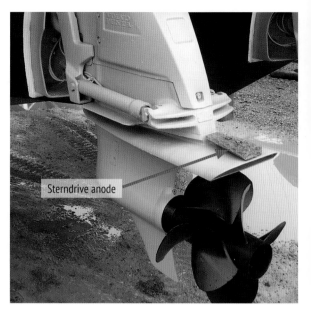

Sterndrive anode

▲ *Flushing ports on sterndrives are quite rare.*

There are a lot of rubber components associated with a sterndrive which are normally immersed in water. If you store your boat on the hard for the winter these rubber components will dry out and they can start to degrade and harden, so it's a good idea to soak the components in a silicone spray, to protect them.

Check the sterndrive anodes. Take them off for the winter period and add new ones for the start of the new season.

Return the sterndrive to the down position when you have finished flushing the raw water and adding the antifreeze to protect the hydraulic 'trim' rams that lift the drive up and down. Having the drive down retracts the ram fully into itself, protecting it from corrosion.

◆ Small, portable outboards

Run the fuel system dry by turning off the fuel while the engine is running until there is no fuel in the system and it stops. Fuel left in the pipes and carburettor will congeal over time if not used.

Flush the raw-water cooling system through with fresh water using a bellows arrangement or a hose fitting.

▲ *Running fresh water through a small outboard engine.*

WASTE OIL

▲ *Waste oil – for oil, diesel and petrol.*

In the case of small outboards, run them in a bucket of fresh water – carefully – with a hose to replenish the water that will spill out of the bucket.

When it comes to small, removable four-stroke outboards and laying them down, you are usually advised to store them on one particular side to stop oil coming out. This is OK for a short time but if stored like this long term then oil can seep past the piston rings and into the exhaust system and when you lift it up oil will come out of the raw-water outlet. Best to leave the outboard stored upright.

Empty the fuel tank on smaller outboard engines as the fuel may go off. Dispose of the old fuel appropriately and fill with fresh fuel (fuel/oil mix) at the start of the season.

◆ Batteries

Make sure wet cells are topped up. Most new batteries are sealed with a glass eye to see the level. Different colour indicates different levels: in good condition, whether it needs a charge or whether it needs replacement.

It's important to make sure the level is correct before charging.

Batteries can explode under load when they are low on electrolyte (sulphuric acid) and the connections to the plates in the battery become corroded. When they come under load a spark is generated, which will ignite the gases produced by the battery charging function. So keep them topped up.

◆ Other areas to check

Rubber parts

You need to look after any rubber components. Alternator belts are best removed for the winter period, which gives you a chance to check not just the belt but also the pulleys, the bearings and to spot corrosion. It also allows the belt to return to its original shape, rather than leaving it in situ under tension. Removing the belt prolongs its life.

We have mentioned the raw-water pump impeller under the raw-water system.

Engine room bilges

Make sure you dry the bilges in the engine room.

Sea cocks

Close all engine room sea cocks. Check their operation and replace any that are corroded.

If leaving a boat in the water, always shut the sea cocks – except any sea cock for a sink that a dehumidifier will be draining into.

Out of the water sea cocks – check condition – and hoses.

Knowing where your sea cocks are is important. A good tip when the boat is out: see how many holes you have and then try and find the relevant sea cocks in the boat.

An oily rag in the exhaust pipe when ashore stops moisture, stops creatures getting in and helps to reduce internal corrosion.

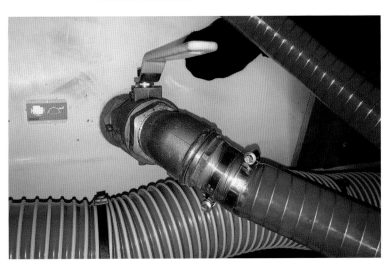

▲ Topped up with distilled water. ▲ Raw-water sea cock.

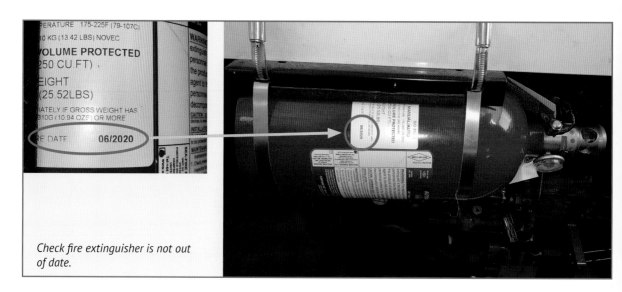

PERATURE 175-225F (79-107C)
0 KG (13.42 LBS) NOVEC
VOLUME PROTECTED
250 CU.FT) ,
EIGHT
(25.52LBS)
ATELY IF GROSS WEIGHT HAS
310G (10.94 OZS) OR MORE

RE DATE   06/2020

Check fire extinguisher is not out of date.

Fresh-water and grey-water holding tanks

Empty them.

Fire extinguishers

Check that they are in date and get them serviced. Fire extinguishers should be serviced annually, now's the time for this.

Alarms

Check fire, gas and carbon monoxide alarms. If battery-powered, check the state and voltage of the battery.

Gas systems

Turn the gas bottle off and disconnect it. Gas inspection – piping lasts 5 years.

▲ *Check fire, gas and carbon monoxide alarms.*

Bilge pumps

Locate the bilge pumps, check that the automatic ones are triggering when their lift float comes on.

Locate shower and toilet pumps and check that they are working.

Heads

Operate the lavatory in the normal way by pumping some sea water into it, then turn off the inlet sea cock and pump the water out of the lavatory. The idea is to have as little sea water left in the pipe from the inlet sea cock to the lavatory as possible. Run some fresh water

Float switch – this turns the bilge pump on automatically when the water level gets to around 2 inches deep

Bilge pump

into the bowl and pump away until the bowl is dry. Shut off the outlet sea cock.

Do this whether you are staying in the water or lifting out.

Windlass

Ease the windlass off. You find mostly that people have the windlass done up drum tight. This puts a dreadful strain on the windlass. So back it off a fraction. Attach the retaining clip or drop nose pin or lashing, whatever you use to make sure your anchor doesn't jump up in the air and start to deploy itself just when you don't want it to. Then with the remote press the down button until the cable – chain or warp – is slack. A quick blip should do it. Or you can do this by hand by unlocking the gypsy and easing the chain out so there is no tension on the windlass. Now you will be giving your windlass a rest for the duration of the winter. Protect the exposed electrical components – the contacts – with a corrosion inhibitor, such as grease or a spray. The contacts may be in the anchor locker or a locker at the forward end of the forecabin.

◈ Damp

Heaters are a great idea for a boat but they don't actually get rid of the moisture. A heater heats up the air and the moisture is absorbed by the warm air and when the air cools the moisture settles out again. Anyone who remembers their weather knows that warm air holds more moisture than cold air, which is why cold fronts travel faster than warm fronts. To get rid of moisture you need a dehumidifier. If you are going to run a dehumidifier when you are not on the boat, do ensure that the discharge pipe leads to a sink that drains outboard and make sure that you have not shut the sea cock off for this drain.

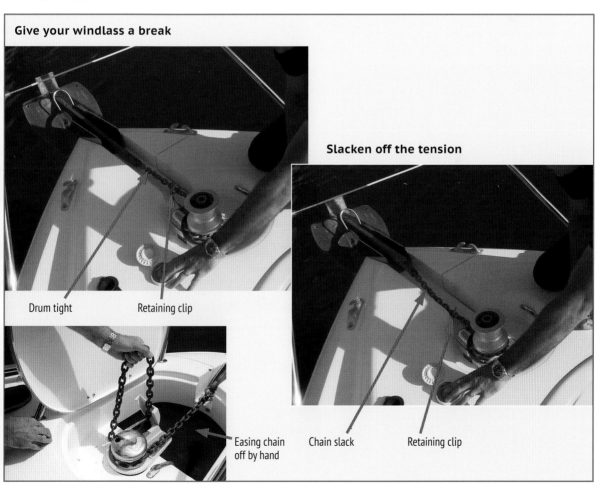

Give your windlass a break

Drum tight   Retaining clip

Easing chain off by hand

Slacken off the tension

Chain slack   Retaining clip

Duncan says: I always keep heat on my boat but cannot afford to run a dehumidifier all the time. I well remember accompanying my friend Bernard on one of his many viewings of boats – the wealthy are always being offered this deal or that – and this day we were to board a beautiful Princess 65. I had always admired the Princess 65 from afar, not just because of its lines but because it was the first modern motorboat that I had seen that had proper bulwarks. These add a measure of safety when walking about the deck, especially the side decks. In my mind, they make a proper boat.

Following Bernard across the bathing platform, through the half-zipped cockpit cover door and then through the patio doors into the saloon, I was struck by how cold it was.

'How much do they want for this boat, Bernard?' He mentioned a Euro Lottery winning sum of money.

'And they can't even be bothered to heat it, to welcome people on board! Bernard, I would not buy this boat!'

'That, Duncan, is because you cannot afford it.'

'True. A bit harsh...'

Warmth makes such a difference. And if you have the money and can afford to run a dehumidifier in conjunction with heaters then that is the best answer, warm and dry.

In fact, the furnishings in a boat that has been kept warm and dry will last longer and so it is very likely that the boat will fetch a better price when it is sold and the investment in electricity for the dehumidifier will have paid off.

Lift cushions off bunks and away from side walls and open lockers and cupboards so that air has a chance to circulate and you don't encourage any damp spots around the boat. Keep the boat aired.

Winterising checklist

Part		Action
Engine		Check fuel system, change filters Change oil and oil filters Check coolant Check and flush raw-water system Check gearbox oil Check stern gland Check bilges clean and dry
Fuel		Check that fuel tank is full
Generator		As for engine
Sea cocks		Closed
Water		Fresh-water tank empty Grey-water tank empty Holding tank empty
Batteries		Checked Topped up
Rubber parts		Lubricated
Gas		Off
Boat		Aired Warm and dry

11 Cautionary tales

When going to sea in any type of vessel, whether it be a rubber dinghy or a superyacht, you must have an understanding of how the sea works, not at a scientific level but at a physical one, and what effect the weather has on it. It must be remembered that a tidal sea is a body of water that goes up and down and moves in many directions; you being on it means you are constantly moving and not being aware of this can lead to a multitude of mistakes when decision-making. It's also prudent to know how the vessel operates – if you do not, bring someone who does. Yes, we all have to start somewhere but not having a person of experience with you can make the sea an unpredictable and dangerous place where making the wrong decisions can lead to one problem being the cause of another, as the following stories will illustrate.

And never set sail without a weather forecast.

It may sound rather critical to say 'every fault on every boat is a result of human error'. But think of any problem you've had with your boat and tell me otherwise. You can even go as far as to say, 'every accident that has ever happened is a result of people's mistakes'. Well, think about it, think about the very last problem you had. What caused it? A lack of concentration, a miscalculation, an engine breakdown, poor communication? What was the root cause of the problem?

I would guess – human error.

Gibraltar Point to North Foreland (5)

Strong winds are forecast

24 hour forecast:

WIND
Northeasterly 3 to 5, occasionally 6 later in northeast, becoming variable 3 or less later in south and east.

SEA STATE
Slight or moderate.

WEATHER
Showers, perhaps thundery, fog patches.

VISIBILITY
Moderate or good, occasionally very poor.

Outlook for the following 24 hours:

WIND
Variable 2 to 4 in south at first, otherwise northeasterly 3 or 4, veering easterly or southeasterly 3 to 5 later.

SEA STATE
Slight, becoming smooth or slight.

WEATHER
Fog patches, thundery showers.

VISIBILITY
Moderate or good, occasionally very poor.

▲ *A neat way of tidying away lines.*

Here are some of the common causes of breakdown.

Jonathan says

Mooring line round the prop

I got a call-out to a chap who said that, while he could start his engine, every time he went to put it in gear the engine stopped.

I asked him if he might have a rope caught round the propeller.

'No,' he replied.

No lines trailing off the boat?

'No.'

Had he picked up a line from a lobster pot? No, he was sailing and moving through the water so not attached to a lobster pot.

I went out to him.

As I approached the yacht and got closer and closer, I could start to make out a line from the bow cleat, running to amidships and under the hull, that was drum tight. Hidden from his view at the helm, he was completely unaware.

He was under sail and I was able to position my workboat alongside and tie on, while the skipper maintained his course. As I jumped from one moving boat to the other, I pointed out to him his line.

'Oh!'

It was the mooring line from the bow cleat, left lying on deck, that had fallen in the water, gone under the hull and was just long enough to get caught on the propeller.

I towed him in and a diver was called to cut the mooring line away.

Moral of the story: always remove mooring lines as soon as you have left the dock. Remove them and put them in a locker where they can do no harm. River boats tend to leave the mooring lines attached but when off the dock skippers will always coil the lines and tidy them away safely. There are a number of clips and hanging systems available but if you really have to leave a line attached, make sure it is short enough so it cannot reach the propeller.

How to free a rope round a prop

In 8 times out of 10 I would reckon to be able to free a rope from a propeller. What you need is an underwater camera and a boathook. Everyone's got a GoPro these days and a selfie stick and if you can see how the rope wrapped itself around the propeller you should be able to unwrap it, as long as it has not become too jammed.

There is no point running the engine in astern to try and free a rope. Normally the rope is caught round the back of the propeller, around the shaft, and as soon as you go into reverse the blades will pick up the rope and wrap it round the other way in front of the propeller and that just makes things worse.

But there is one thing you can do and that is to get the rope off the propeller with the boathook so you have the rope on the shaft, with the free end, the running end, out one side and the fixed end, the standing end, out the other side and then you turn the propeller.

You do this by starting the engine in gear but with the fuel shut-off lever lifted or the stop button pressed in, so the engine doesn't start but cranks and turns over. This will turn the propeller slowly. Turning one way will tighten the rope and turning the other way will unravel the rope. Find out which way will release the rope and then little by little crank the engine until the rope is free.

Other than that, it is a matter of calling out the divers – dive master, a diver and a dive buddy – a cast of three, which is best done back on the berth in the marina.

'My engine gearbox has jammed and I need help quickly as I am in the way of the ferries.'

It was blowing a good 25 knots from the south-east. I was coming from the River Hamble straight into the wind and sea. I was going to get wet. As I left the river and headed east, the strong breeze hit me along with the spray. I made 25 knots to Gilkicker Point, which in the lumpy sea involved a lot of slamming and plenty of water over the boat. With waves pounding the front of the boat, trying to get a balance between the best speed and the least damage to the boat is a skill I've developed over the years. As I rounded the point, I started getting hit by larger waves of about 1.5 metres and being single-handed I realised that it might prove difficult to try and fix the yacht out here. I planned for a 'tow in' and called the casualty for an updated location. No answer. There were a few yachts out there. I made my way to one directly ahead. Was this the casualty? No. I was now battling through large waves. Where was the casualty? I tried the radio and phone again. Still no answer. I then saw two yachts, one to my port making its way under sail into Portsmouth, one to my starboard one mile away. I headed to the one to port. As I approached, I got a call:

'I can see you, You're going away from us!' Ah, the casualty was the yacht to starboard. They had their sails set and as I got close, I decided that it might be best to escort the vessel into the harbour under sail rather than to attempt a tow.

I explained my plan to the skipper and he started to head towards Portsmouth. The Wootton ferry was coming in from one direction, the Brittany ferry from another direction and a fast cat was coming out. Our 5 knots would put us right in the centre of these three, so I advised the casualty to go about and wait until the danger had passed. There was a big sea running and it was hard for each of us to hold our bow into the wind and waves. Eventually, with all the ferries out of the way, we turned in for Portsmouth. With the sea on the stern we were both being slewed all over the place and it was hard going. So it took a little over an hour after arriving on scene until we entered Portsmouth harbour. In the protection of the harbour I was able to tie on to the casualty and tow her on to a pontoon berth in the marina.

'Right, let's see if we can fix the problem. Tell me again, what happened? I understand the gearbox is jammed?' I said.

'Well yes, I think so. I couldn't move the gear lever from forward to neutral to start the engine,' was the reply.

'You know what? I wouldn't be at all surprised if the problem hasn't fixed itself,' I said, without even touching the controls. I then went to the lever and sure enough, it was free to move in and out of gear. We started the engine and all was well. The customer was holding his head in disbelief.

'You have a fixed, rather than folding prop, don't you, sir,' I said. The skipper nodded.

'Well, if you sail with a fixed prop and put it in gear to stop the prop spinning, the pressure of the water flowing against the propeller can bind the gears in the gearbox together so tightly that the gear linkage cannot release the gearbox into neutral. But just by slowing your speed, or going about, or even starting the engine, it can be released instantly.'

Lesson learned: Know your engine, know your setup, fixed prop, folding prop and what can happen when you lock them off. Yes, you can start the diesel engine on most yachts when it's in gear.

▲ Conditions off Portsmouth.

▲ This wasn't the yacht in the story but you get the idea.

Bump start

One of the Sea Start lads got called out to a fishing boat in Christchurch Bay whose starter motor had packed up. It had a fixed prop and it needed to be towed in. It was low water at Christchurch so it needed to be towed about 20 miles to Poole.

And just for the hell of it he suggested leaving the engine in gear.

And then he towed the fishing boat as hard as he could.

And lo and behold the engine started.

So you can bump start a boat, but not always. I have not tried the technique myself but it's worth a try and if you are going to have a go, follow the points below. Of course, once the boat starts, as it is in gear, the propeller will start to drive the boat so someone must be at the helm ready to control the boat.

You don't need the ignition to be on to get the engine to turn over and start. But you do need the ignition on to turn on the instruments and their associated lights.

You also need the ignition on to energise the alternator. If the ignition is off, despite the fact that the drive belt will be turning, the alternator will not be charging the batteries as it needs to be energised. A signal from the ignition energises the windings in the alternator, which then start the charging process.

So if you are going to try a bump start under tow, put the engine into gear and turn the ignition on. You will just have to live with the alternator charging alarm sound until the engine catches, when it will turn off.

What a waste

There was a chap – a few years ago – with a twin-engine motorboat who had an engine blow up as he left Cowes on his way to Portsmouth. He was so cross that this had happened that he drove flat out to Portsmouth on the remaining good engine and blew that one up too. We towed him up to Port Solent. The boat was lifted and he was quoted £60,000 to replace both engines. I don't know the rest of the story but the boat has been on the hard ever since. Seems sad really.

Can't start the engine

Very early in the morning, a call came in from a skipper in the west country with a big twin-engine boat saying he couldn't start one of the engines. We wouldn't get out to him being that far away but would call in another engineer in the area, although it was a bit early for this. So I tried to see what I could do over the phone.

He said the engine had started fine three weeks ago.

'What sort of engine?'

'A Caterpillar.'

'What happens?'

'The engine turns over but does not fire.'

Caterpillars of that size have a stop button that you push to stop the engine, rather than a pull lever. This cuts off the compressed fuel going to the engine. The stop button has a solenoid and this pushes a lever that cuts the fuel off. I told him what to look for and which side of the engine it was on and he went into the engine room to have a look.

He came back to report that he had fixed it. He keeps an oil-fired heater between the engines to keep the engine bay warm all year round and this had fallen over on the lever and was preventing it from moving, so it was still in the off position and no fuel was getting to the engine. Moving the oil-fired heater meant the solenoid was operating correctly and he was able to start the engine.

You can do quite a lot in terms of talking people through an operation.

Rope round the prop – serious and not so serious

It was late afternoon on a Sunday and I got a call to attend a casualty, anchored in Studland Bay. They had a sports boat and they had got a rope caught round the propeller and they needed to free it to get home.

By the time I got there from Warsash it was about 6pm. I noticed they had a stern drive. I said, 'Can't you just lift the stern drive and take the rope off?'

'Oh, I hadn't thought of that.'

'Don't worry, I'll do it.' I noticed the water was quite shallow so rather than get the RIB near the sharp propeller I got into the water. It was only about a metre deep and it was mid-summer.

He raised the leg of the stern drive and I just unwound the rope from the propeller and got back into the RIB.

It was 30 miles to get to him, a round trip for me of 60 miles. He had been swimming round the boat that afternoon. For some reason, he didn't realise he could raise the leg.

He did look a little bit sheepish.

It was the people on the boats next to us who were laughing, that I had been called out to do something so simple. Mind you, it was a fine day, flat calm and it had been a lovely run down to Studland Bay.

For some reason, when things go wrong or the unexpected happens, some people lose all common sense and panic. People today go straight to Google to see how to do something and if they can't understand it will just call for help rather than looking at the problem and thinking how they might solve it themselves.

It's a bit like a satnav. They are really good but if it packs up and someone asks you how you got from A to B you wouldn't have a clue because the satnav had just been telling you where to go and you probably weren't paying attention.

Mooring buoy caught around prop

A colleague of mine was called to a yacht in the Solent trying to get back to Ocean Village Marina in Southampton. Now the yacht had an issue with the engine cutting out. It would restart but it cut out every time it was put in gear. This always suggests a fouled propeller.

The skipper would need help once he reached the entrance to Ocean Village to moor but was quite happy to sail up Southampton Water to save us having to tow all the way. However, we still like to escort the vessel to the point it is safe to come alongside and take over the tow, so my colleague headed out and met the yacht. The tide was on the ebb but not running fast and the winds favourable for sailing but progress was slow, so slow in fact that after a while it was decided to tow the vessel from ahead to speed up the rescue. It was towed into Ocean Village Marina and on to its mooring.

Now, when my colleague got back to the office, he explained everything that had gone on and said, 'That was a tow and a half, it took ages to get that yacht in.'

'Was it big, the tide wasn't that strong,' I said.

'It was a 50-footer but it just didn't like being towed. I mean, I was flat out only doing about 3 knots. And when I reached Ocean Village and swapped from a forward tow to alongside, the boat was all over the place!' he said.

'What was the issue?' I asked.

'It didn't want to go around corners and I swear it felt like I was stuck to the ground at some point,' he said.

All was explained when the next day we had a call from the divers who we called out to check the propeller. When they went under the boat, they saw a rope attached to the prop, which was attached to a chain, which was attached to a concrete block! The skipper had only gone and picked up a mooring buoy, complete with sinker, from a local sailing club and it must have been swinging from the prop in deeper water but acting like an anchor once it reached shallower waters.

Forgot to open the sea cock

It's an easy mistake to make but forgetting to put your sea cock on can get you into all sorts of bother, because forgetting a simple thing will lead to other problems, which will escalate quickly.

I am reminded of a Mayday call to a yacht we overheard on the radio one day, reporting a fire on board. A fire on board is a serious issue and we listened intently as the Coastguard coordinated a rescue with the RNLI. The vessel was towed into the River Hamble and left on a mooring near our office. Shortly after this we received a call from the boatowner, asking if we could help fix his boat.

'Has the engine fire done much damage?' I asked.

He was surprised I knew of the issue and realised that it had been broadcast over the airwaves.

'In fact the RNLI had a look and realised there were no flames but the engine smells of burning rubber,' he said.

We signed the skipper up as a member of our organisation and went over to see what we could do.

The skipper was clearly shaken up and the other sailors were stressed and at the time had clearly been terrified that the boat was on fire.

Looking around the engine, I soon found that the rubber exhaust pipe on the back of the engine and the plastic exhaust water lock had been severely heat damaged. This is a sure indication of a lack of cooling water to keep the exhaust temperature down, which suggested that the raw-water system was blocked.

So, the obvious thing was to try and find the cause of the blockage and the first thing we check is ... did you guess it?

Correct ... the sea cock, which was in the closed position!

'Oh $%£$^%$££$%!' was the skipper's reaction to the news.

Remember, leaving the sea cock off or closed, and as a result overheating the engine and exhaust, will mean that the system has to be carefully checked and normally the work involved is:

1. Remove and replace the damaged impeller and shaft seal as both will be heat damaged. Find all the disintegrated parts of the impeller so they do not block the water ways or heat exchanger.
2. The coolant normally expresses itself due to the engine overheating, which results in over-expansion of the coolant, creating excess pressure in the system. This then sprays off the coolant pressure cap. So, new coolant for topping up is required and a clean-up of the old expressed coolant, which will have covered the engine and engine bay.
3. Replace the damaged exhaust pipe and water lock.

Time-consuming and expensive.

But the whole thing could have been avoided by simply having a reminder that the sea cock was closed. You cannot see sea cocks and they can easily get forgotten. Having a pre-sailing checklist could have prevented this breakdown.

Forgot to put fuel on

This is another common issue that can occur if you are in the habit of shutting off your fuel, or perhaps if an engineer has just been working on the engine. Their best practice is to leave the boat safe, which may involve shutting the fuel off, whereas you may tend to leave the fuel on. They should of course let you know that the fuel has been shut off.

But this story is not about that; in fact, it is about a client who attended one of my diesel-engine courses. He had spent the whole day listening attentively and according to him had learned a great deal all of which he was going to put into action. Another satisfied customer.

He called me the next day to say he was out on his boat and the engine wasn't revving fully. 'I didn't learn as much as I thought,' he said. 'I have looked around and cannot see any issues. I'm sure it's going to be expensive.'

'Don't worry, I'm nearby, I will come and have a look.'

Now, the reason that an engine will fail to rev will be because of an issue with the fuel, so the first and easiest thing to check, as taught on the course, is to make sure the fuel is on properly.

'Well, the shut-off handle is half off,' he said when I got there.

'That will do it,' I said, turning it back on fully.

'Oh,' was the response. 'I could have done that.'

'It's easily done, don't worry, but always check the simplest thing first,' I repeated from my course the day before.

On closer inspection, the fuel shut-off handle was very light to move. It was mounted horizontally so it was open in the 3 o'clock position and to turn it off you moved it down clockwise by 90 degrees to 6 o'clock. So, it was actually starting to turn itself off as the owner went over the waves. The simple fix was to loosen the fuel tap and reposition it so that the handle had to go up to turn off. That way, gravity would not play a part any more.

It is a lesson in checking the obvious first and being methodical. Most solutions to breakdowns are simple.

Running out of fuel

Now, this is a fairly common call-out. Believe it or not, it is normally a fault with the fuel gauge that causes people to run out of fuel, they can be unreliable, inaccurate and optimistic. When a boat is new to you, always make the gauge prove its worth, never trust it is accurate.

One reason for running out of fuel can be lack of communication. This proved to be the case when I was called out to a chartered RIB, which over the space of a few days started with the gauge reading half full and had ended up reading full, when the RIB broke down. No one had twigged that the gauge was reading backwards and each person using the RIB thought the one before had topped up the fuel as the gauge was higher each time they used it! The fuel sender unit, it turned out, had been replaced with the incorrect type the day before the charter.

But you can also run out of fuel due to bad planning, basically not having enough fuel for the journey you have planned. A good but interesting example of this was a call I received, just as the sun went down one evening, to a sports boat, which had run out of fuel just about half a mile off the River Hamble entrance, I jumped on my workboat and headed out in the dark. It was a breezy evening and the location of the boat meant that it was being blown on to the shore quite quickly, On my approach I could see the lights of the boat and it was very close to the shoreline. Being very shallow, I tentatively worked my way over to him with a strong breeze and waves pushing my boat towards the shore. As I got over to them it was very dark, I could not make the boat out very well but I could see it broadside to the shore, the beach being just behind, but somehow the boat was not aground. 'How could this be?' I thought to myself. I lit up my floodlight and to my amazement saw a floating pontoon half on the beach with the speedboat moored perfectly alongside it!

Not sure of the situation, I contacted the speedboat owner and the answer was:

'It's my pontoon, I have just picked it up and was towing it back to my berth. I didn't realise how much fuel I would use towing the bleeding thing!'

It was not easy to get a line across to them as every time I left the helm to throw a line, the sea pushed my boat almost on top of them and I had to back off several times for safety.

Unbelievably, even though we were on a remote part of the beach, some joggers running past stopped to ask if they could help. One even took a line from me and walked it to the speedboat.

I was able to gingerly turn the workboat around and start to pull the speedboat off the shore on a long tow line. The speedboat then started to tow the pontoon also on a long tow line. I slowly towed both the speedboat and pontoon into the river and managed to get both on to a very long visitor pontoon.

Everyone was much relieved. Then we saw the funny side and incredibly the lucky side of things, that he just happened to be blown on to his own dock that he was towing by chance, which had stopped the boat from running aground and which enabled a much easier rescue.

I put a few gallons of fuel in the speedboat, got the engine started and sent them on their way, up to their mooring further up the river.

So, plan your trips carefully and always put in more than enough fuel for whatever journey you are undertaking.

Bilge full of water

Bilges that fill up with water can be the result of a number of things, rainwater, leaking stern glands, leaking domestic water pipes, sea cocks leaking, poorly sealed skin fittings. They can also be a result of not de-winterising your boat.

The last reason may seem odd but winterising your engine involves different techniques depending on your engine type and this story is the result of not knowing what winterising your engine entails. You see, in this story, the engine had been winterised by an engineer and come the spring and the first sunny day of the year the owner thought he would take his inboard-petrol-engine speedboat out for a spin. But instead of checking it was ready to go, he simply jumped aboard, started it up, dropped the lines and went off down the river.

I was actually standing on a pontoon in the same river at the time and saw the speedboat turn around at the end of the river and come back in. As it passed, I could see water pumping out of the back by the bilge pump outlet, the engine bay was up and the skipper looked worried. I headed over to him and saw the engine was full of water. He turned the engine off and slowly the level started to drop. I helped with a bilge pump we keep on the workboat and soon emptied it out.

Not knowing where the leak was coming from but now with the engine and the water level having dropped, I assumed the water was being pumped in by the engine. On closer inspection I realised that the drains for the exhaust manifold, water pump and engine block had been removed, which meant that the raw water would not be exiting the boat via the exhaust but would be pumped straight into the bilges. Removing the drains is something an engineer would do to winterise this type of engine to protect it from freezing damage and corrosion. The engineer should have notified the owner and the owner should have understood his engine better.

Always carry out engine checks before any trip. This could have been easily avoided by checking the engine before starting and after starting or by just picking up the phone to the engineer to see what he had done for the winterising. The boat could easily have sunk and doing these basic simple checks would have saved the owner a lot of stress and heartache in the long run.

Missing engine part

Doing an engine check – water, oil, battery, belt, leaks, nothing fallen off, exhaust – before every journey is always important, never more so than with this story.

It was a Saturday morning and we received a call from a man who was experiencing a loss of power in his port engine.

He had left his pontoon, run down the river and when he got out into open water, he had opened up the throttles but the port engine did not speed up; in fact, all he got from it was a huge cloud of black exhaust smoke. He quickly turned round, headed back to his mooring and called us.

The report of black smoke from the engine indicated a possible lack of turbo pressure. The black smoke is a result of an imbalance in the ratio of diesel to air. As the throttle opens and more fuel is pumped to the cylinders, this is balanced by an increase in the air that comes from the turbo. If there is something wrong with the turbo, this extra air is missing and the excess fuel is burnt inefficiently and creates black smoke.

I climbed into the engine bay and had a good look round the Volvo Penta KAD300 diesel engine. I was particularly interested to see the condition of a solid metal pipe that goes between the turbo and the intercooler and the fixing clips, because it is fairly common for them to corrode and come loose.

'Er, it's missing!' I said out loud.

'What's missing?' was the response.

'The pipe from the turbo is missing. I can't see it anywhere,' I said.

'Well it can't be far away, maybe it's under the engine,' the owner said, trying to be helpful.

I looked behind the engine, under it and next to it but the pipe was nowhere to be seen. This was bizarre, I mean the pipe is a foot long and 2 inches wide, it's hard to miss!

I finally came up for air and as I looked up out of the engine bay, I noticed a ledge above the engine and there on this ledge was the pipe and neatly placed next to it was the jubilee clip.

After pointing this out to the owner, he took me through the recent engineering history of the boat and the story started to come together. An engineer had been instructed to replace a sensor on the engine. However, he had let the owner down several times by not turning up to do the work when he said he would. A practice that is very common in the marine industry and understandably the owner, frustrated by this, decided to get a new engineer and cancelled the old one. The new engineer was booked to come in a few days' time. In the meantime, the owner had been using the boat, because although the engine needed a new sensor it had always run perfectly well without it. He had last used it two days before and everything had been fine.

So, somehow this pipe must have been removed within the last two days.

'I would call the original engineer,' I said.

After a lengthy discussion, some heated words and an abrupt end to the conversation, the full explanation came out. The old engineer decided that he had let the owner down when finally he was told he wasn't needed any more. So, he decided to go that day to the boat to fix the problem but didn't tell the owner he was attending. Once he was on board, he took off the pipe to access the sensor he needed to replace. But then realising he had the wrong part, he decided to leave, order the part and wait to fit it a couple of days later, leaving the engine in pieces. He didn't tell the owner or leave a note to say the engine was unusable. Nothing.

As far as the owner was concerned, he had cancelled the first engineer and that was that. And today, completely unaware that the turbo was no longer connected to the port engine, he had taken the boat out for a run around.

Always do your engine checks, and remember to look 'up' as well as down when checking whether any parts have fallen off your engine. You never can be too sure!

Net attached to yacht

I got a call to attend a yacht off the entrance to Portsmouth harbour along the wall at Haslar. They were reporting a fouled propeller. I came alongside, introduced myself and then dropped a camera under the water to see what was caught on the propeller. It was a fishing net. I couldn't see the end of it but it was well tangled up in the prop.

The skipper had already contacted the Coastguard so I told them I was in attendance and giving assistance. The yacht was at anchor so I decided to get a boathook, haul in the net and cut it away shorter so I could tow the yacht alongside. I would need to do this to bring it to a berth, without the net tangling up in my own propeller.

I managed to hook the net and pull it partly aboard. Attaching it to my towing post, I pulled it in tight to the propeller, made it as short as possible and cut it away. I then tried to haul in the rest of the net but it was very long and I soon realised that about 100 metres away a small floating buoy was heading towards me. In fact, there were several floats in a row, all heading towards me.

▲ *Hauling in the small buoy.*

▲ *The net!*

Aware that I still had a yacht, with the cut away part of the net around its prop, which I had to tow in, I decided to call the Coastguard back and inform them the net was a hazard and needed recovery. Their rather unhelpful response was to ask me to pull it in myself so as not to endanger any other boats. 'Ok, I will haul it in if I can,' I said.

I tied the workboat alongside the yacht, and then started to haul the net in. The floats came towards me but then it became very hard to pull it in any more. I noticed that the yacht's anchor chain was drum tight and I needed more slack to get the net in. So, I decided to let the net out again and pull up the yacht's anchor. This allowed me to haul in the net. Basically, I was pulling the yacht and my workboat through the water. I finally got to what I thought was the end of the net, but it was anchored to the ground. I tugged it as hard as I could. Luckily, it came free. It had a piece of scrap metal on the end as a weight, an anchor, and as I pulled it out a new line appeared going off at 90 degrees in the other direction. I still hadn't reached the end of the net. I kid you not, I carried on pulling and the amount of net I gathered in was tremendous. It had dead fish in it, crabs, debris and mud all over it as I hauled it in, still pulling the two boats as I went. Finally, up to my thighs in net and exhausted, the last of it came aboard.

I got a round of applause from the crew of the yacht as they stared in amazement at the amount of net aboard. Then I towed them back into Portsmouth harbour where a lift out was arranged to clear the prop.

Here is a picture of the net. Piled into a trolley, you don't really get an idea of just how long it was.

Aground

When a boat runs aground it's important to consider the seabed that it has run aground on. Mud is forgiving, sand and shells less so, pebbles are not good and worst of all is rock. The wave motion as the tide ebbs will give the boat a nasty workout on any rock. If you can free yourself before the tide runs out, so much the better. Sailing boats have the option of getting the crew to hang off the boom to heel the boat. Motorboats do not have this option. Worse, their props may be exposed and the first thing to make contact with the seabed.

I had a phone call from a yacht between Alum Bay and the Needles. The skipper had gone really close into shore, dropped his anchor and now the tide was going out he realised he was aground. It was a fin keel 40-foot yacht and he was literally 150 metres from the cliffs and it is really rocky there. Just as he saw it was getting shallower, he tried to get the anchor but he couldn't move it. He then realised that not only were the rocks between him and the shore, there were also rocks between him and the deeper water. So he called us to say he'd run aground. It took me about half an hour from the call to getting there, and by the time I got to him he was solidly aground with the boat about 20cm (8 inches) out of the water and just starting to heel.

I could see that the anchor was jammed in the rocks. The boat was actually lying on sand but there were rocks either side of it and as the tide went out and it leaned right over so it would come into contact with the rocks. An added problem was that there were ten people on this boat. And of course, being only a small RIB, I couldn't get everyone on board. So the crew would have to remain on the yacht.

Being well aground, I couldn't tow the boat forwards or backwards. The only thing to do was to tow it sideways but from the top of the mast to reduce the draught.

The first thing to do was to get the anchor, which was jammed under a rock. I couldn't get it up so I asked them to let it go and buoy the chain.

We then got the spinnaker halyard and attached it to the tow rope. And you don't need a lot of power to get the mast to come over and the boat to heel. On the first try it came over but the boat didn't come off the sand, so I adjusted the angle and I tried again and again, each time trying not to pull too hard. Remember, the tide was going out all the time. Finally, I pulled really hard and the boat came over about 60 degrees, the port rail went underwater and the crew were hanging on for dear life, but the boat popped up and over the rocks and was afloat once more.

So, with them off the skipper said, 'Thanks for that. What about my anchor?'

I asked him to get the engine going and suggested he motor off and I went back for the anchor. I got hold of the fender and pulled all the chain on to the RIB. I tied some chain to the tow bar and worked it one way and then the other and eventually it came free. By now they were about 3 miles away so I went over and handed them their anchor.

'Oh, thanks for that. Bye.'

Sometimes you don't get much by way of thanks for getting them out of a fix.

How to troubleshoot a breakdown

Flow charts

The best way to troubleshoot breakdowns is via flow charts and here are some of the common issues that you will come across and how you might get to the bottom of what has gone wrong and fix it, or at least know what has to be fixed.

These flow diagrams are the result of thousands of call-outs over many years and while they don't cover every single eventuality, they cover the most common ones. If your issue is not covered here then it will be a rare issue that you may need professional help to solve.

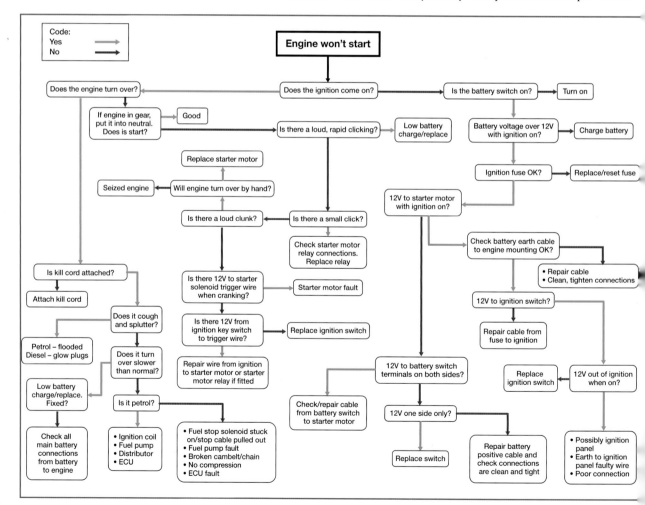

How to turn the engine over

▶ *A spanner on the crankshaft pulley nut will do it.*

▲ *Decompression levers down – normal engine operation mode.*

▲ *Decompression levers up – releasing compression and allowing you to turn the engine over.*

▲ *Full stop out – fuel off.*

▲ *Full stop in – fuel on.*

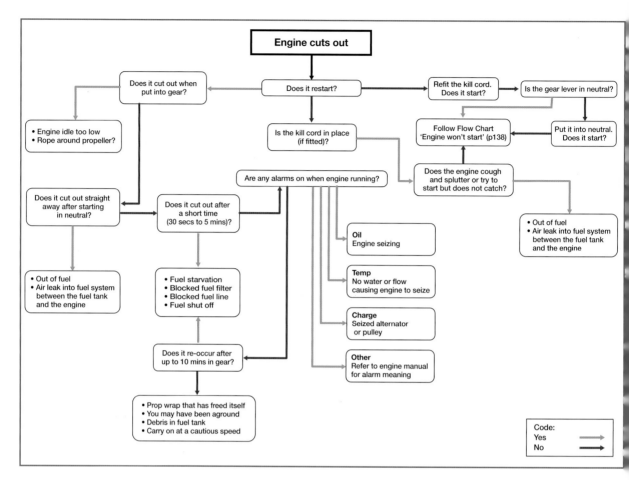

Engine cuts out

You will see in the flow diagram above that one of the reasons your engine may have cut out but, having re-started, is now running fine, is that you have momentarily been aground. This will have stopped the propeller from turning and the engine will have stopped. Now, afloat, the propeller is able to turn unimpeded. You might think that this was outrageous, 'How can anyone have run their boat aground and not noticed?' Well, as we said at the start, all of these situations have been encountered when out helping on breakdowns and running aground without being aware of it is not as unusual as you might think. Do make sure your depth sounder is calibrated and working and keep a good eye on it.

Of course, if you do have a grounding and are aware of it then it is prudent to get your boat lifted and checked by a surveyor for damage to the keel (fin keels, bulb keels, wing keels especially), the stern gear (rudder), props and prop shafts.

Engine overheating

Be careful, when dealing with a hot engine, that you do not burn yourself. Heavy-duty gloves will help and you can check the temperature of everything with that infrared thermometer that we recommended you get in Chapter 4. Never remove the coolant-pressure cap when the engine is hot as it will be under pressure. Allow the engine to cool before removal and place a towel over the cap when removing just in case there is still pressure in the system.

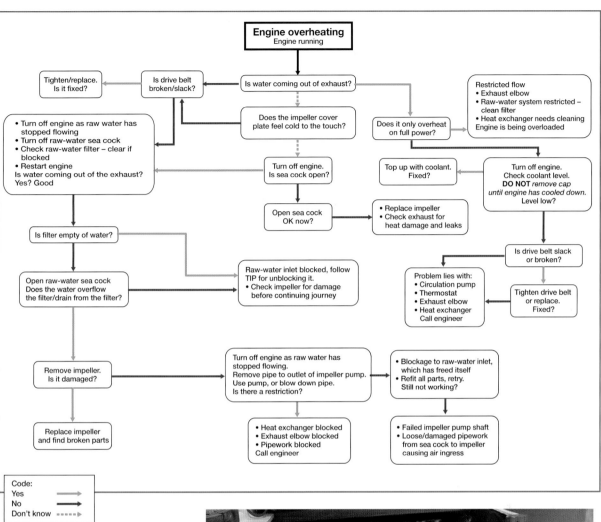

Engine overheating
Engine running

↓

Is water coming out of exhaust?

Is drive belt broken/slack?
→ Tighten/replace. Is it fixed?

Does the impeller cover plate feel cold to the touch?

Does it only overheat on full power?

Restricted flow
• Exhaust elbow
• Raw-water system restricted – clean filter
• Heat exchanger needs cleaning
Engine is being overloaded

• Turn off engine as raw water has stopped flowing
• Turn off raw-water sea cock
• Check raw-water filter – clear if blocked
• Restart engine
Is water coming out of the exhaust?
Yes? Good

Turn off engine. Is sea cock open?

Top up with coolant. Fixed?

Turn off engine. Check coolant level. DO NOT *remove cap until engine has cooled down.* Level low?

Open sea cock OK now?

• Replace impeller
• Check exhaust for heat damage and leaks

Is filter empty of water?

Raw-water inlet blocked, follow TIP for unblocking it.
• Check impeller for damage before continuing journey

Is drive belt slack or broken?

Open raw-water sea cock Does the water overflow the filter/drain from the filter?

Problem lies with:
• Circulation pump
• Thermostat
• Exhaust elbow
• Heat exchanger
Call engineer

Tighten drive belt or replace. Fixed?

Remove impeller. Is it damaged?

Turn off engine as raw water has stopped flowing. Remove pipe to outlet of impeller pump. Use pump, or blow down pipe. Is there a restriction?

• Blockage to raw-water inlet, which has freed itself
• Refit all parts, retry. Still not working?

Replace impeller and find broken parts

• Heat exchanger blocked
• Exhaust elbow blocked
• Pipework blocked
Call engineer

• Failed impeller pump shaft
• Loose/damaged pipework from sea cock to impeller causing air ingress

Code:
Yes →
No →
Don't know ·····▸

▲ *Coolant midway between max and min, ideal.*

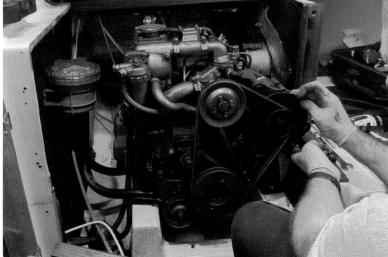

▲ *If you can turn the alternator and the drive belt slides round the crankshaft and circulation pump without turning them then the belt is too loose.*

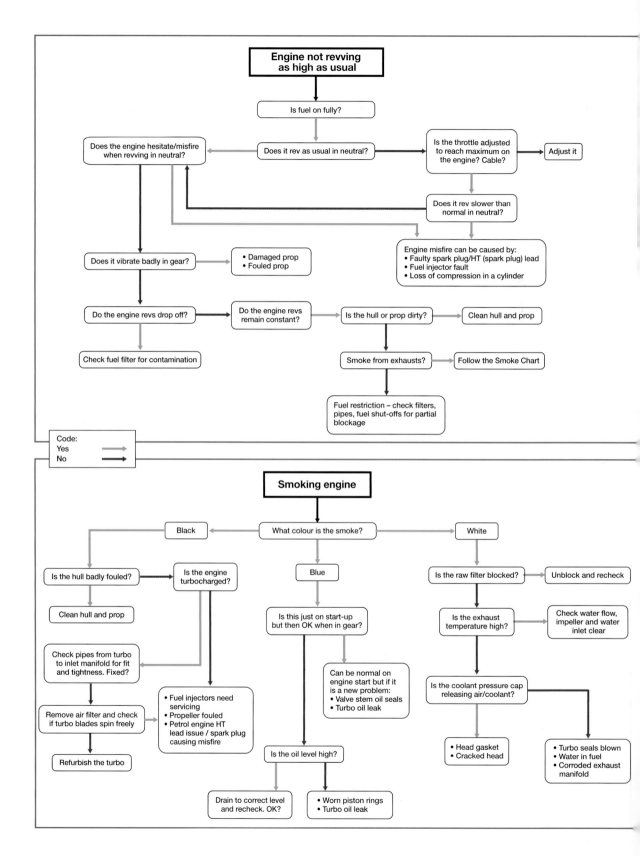

Engine not revving as high as usual

Is fuel on fully?

Does the engine hesitate/misfire when revving in neutral? ← Does it rev as usual in neutral? → Is the throttle adjusted to reach maximum on the engine? Cable? → Adjust it

Does it rev slower than normal in neutral?

Does it vibrate badly in gear? →
- Damaged prop
- Fouled prop

Engine misfire can be caused by:
- Faulty spark plug/HT (spark plug) lead
- Fuel injector fault
- Loss of compression in a cylinder

Do the engine revs drop off? → Do the engine revs remain constant? → Is the hull or prop dirty? → Clean hull and prop

Check fuel filter for contamination

Smoke from exhausts? → Follow the Smoke Chart

Fuel restriction – check filters, pipes, fuel shut-offs for partial blockage

Code:
Yes →
No →

Smoking engine

What colour is the smoke?

Black ← What colour is the smoke? → White

Is the hull badly fouled? → Is the engine turbocharged?

Blue

Is the raw filter blocked? → Unblock and recheck

Clean hull and prop

Is this just on start-up but then OK when in gear?

Is the exhaust temperature high? → Check water flow, impeller and water inlet clear

Check pipes from turbo to inlet manifold for fit and tightness. Fixed?

Can be normal on engine start but if it is a new problem:
- Valve stem oil seals
- Turbo oil leak

Is the coolant pressure cap releasing air/coolant?

- Fuel injectors need servicing
- Propeller fouled
- Petrol engine HT lead issue / spark plug causing misfire

Remove air filter and check if turbo blades spin freely

Refurbish the turbo

Is the oil level high?

- Head gasket
- Cracked head

- Turbo seals blown
- Water in fuel
- Corroded exhaust manifold

Drain to correct level and recheck. OK?

- Worn piston rings
- Turbo oil leak

KNOW YOUR SMOKE

White smoke – water in the exhaust, so hot that it has become steam.
This will be either:

- Too little water passing through the exhaust, caused by a blockage in the raw-water cooling system.
- Water leaking into the exhaust as a result of damage to the engine. This is the more serious of the two and can be caused by anything from a cracked exhaust manifold to a cylinder-head gasket failure.

Black smoke – inefficient burning of the diesel by the engine.

- Overloading the engine causes more fuel to be fed to the cylinders – as the engine tries to deliver the power – than the available air can burn. Black smoke is the unburnt fuel in the exhaust. The most common causes of overloading are a dirty hull or a lot of barnacles on the propeller.
- Where an injector is not injecting the fuel properly because it is damaged or leaking, creating a bad spray pattern that prevents the fuel from burning properly.
- If the engine is turbocharged you could be losing pressured air between the turbo and the engine. There could be an air leak from the turbo, which would mean you would not get the correct amount of air into the engine that it was designed to receive, so the fuel to air ratio might be wrong. With more fuel than air, the extra diesel would burn off as black smoke.

Blue smoke – oil in the exhaust.
Most diesel engines will burn a little oil when they start. This disappears after a short while. If it continues, it shows that you have a lot of engine wear – an old engine. Excess wear erodes the piston rings and the cylinder walls, creating a gap just big enough for the lubricating oil, which is sprayed up under the piston, to pass the piston rings and burn in the combustion chamber. A compression test will tell you if this is the case.

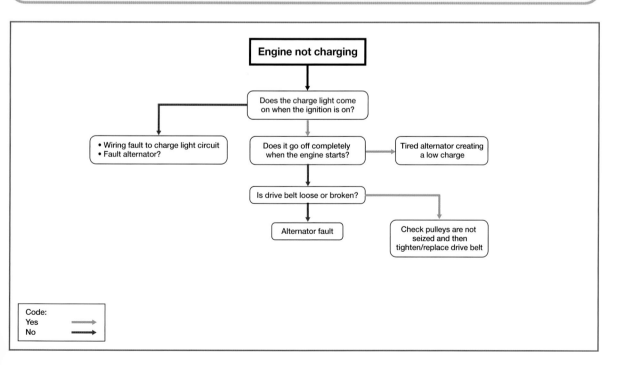

Diagnosing common problems

◆ Poor fuel economy

Normally, poor fuel economy is down to hull and prop condition. If you are still experiencing poor fuel economy with a clean bottom, check for excessive smoke and follow the 'smoking engine' flow diagram. Additionally, have a look around the engine and the engine bay for any obvious fuel leaks. If you have a turbo fitted, check to see if there could be any air pressure losses in this area, the easiest way is to raise the engine speed and you will hear and feel the air escaping around the pipes and joints from the turbo to the inlet manifold. If you are still concerned then turn to a professional for advice on what the fuel economy should be and changes that could be made to the fuel system and even propeller changes to help improve the economy.

◆ Carburettor malfunctions

Poor starting, idling and an engine dropping revs and then picking up speed (hunting) can be caused by an issue with the carburettor. You can clean out the carburettor yourself but certainly don't do it for the first time without someone showing you how to do it. You can easily damage gaskets and small internal parts. Also, unless you know what parts to clean, you will probably not clean or repair the part that is causing the issue.

◆ Engine runs poorly at idle

This can be caused by the idle speed being slightly low. Check in the owner's manual what the speed should be. You can adjust the idle speed on most diesel engines. If you have a petrol engine and it has a carburettor, the air/fuel mix can be adjusted so the engine runs more smoothly. If it is running too rich (more fuel than required) then it may be fouling the spark plugs, which will make the engine struggle to run at idle and stall. If it is a petrol fuel-injected engine then the fuel mixture and idle speed is controlled by an engine management system so there is no adjustment for fuel and air as the EMS will do this for you. If, however, it still does not idle correctly, this may indicate a fault with the 'idle speed control valve', which controls the amount of air allowed to mix with the fuel at idle speed. This can gum up with oily deposits that hold dirt and may just need cleaning. This is a job for an engineer.

◆ Oil pressure

The oil-pressure gauge on your instrument panel will alert you to low oil pressure and if the oil-pressure switch is triggered an alarm will sound. If you don't have an oil-pressure gauge you will simply get an alarm when the oil pressure is too low. It is very important that if you lose oil pressure the engine is turned off straight away as internal engine damage will be occurring. It can take as little as two minutes with no oil pressure for an engine to seize.

◆ Excessive oil consumption

Unless you have an obvious oil leak there is rarely a simple reason for this and it usually takes extensive engine work to resolve. The most common cause of excessive oil usage is a tired engine with worn-out parts that allow oil to pass into the combustion chamber via the piston rings, which is then burnt through the engine and results in blue smoke from the exhaust at all engine speeds.

◆ Engine speeds up for no apparent reason

Engines only speed up for no apparent reason for two reasons:
1. If the engine has been starved of the full fuel supply, which has then cleared, allowing the engine to reach the correct revs. If it slows down again, then the partial blockage has returned.
2. If a load has been taken off the engine. If you are in gear, motoring along gently and a following sea gives you a helpful shove, then a load will be taken off the engine and the revs might increase momentarily.

◆ Troubleshooting small petrol outboard engines

When you have finished using your outboard engine:
1. Turn off the fuel and run the engine until it stops. You do not want to leave it with petrol in the system. The petrol can go off and or congeal if it has oil in it and this will clog the carburettor.
2. Run the outboard through with fresh water to clean the raw-water cooling system and prevent salt deposits.
3. Empty the fuel tank if you are leaving the outboard for some time, such as over the winter.

Follow these flow diagrams for other common outboard problems.

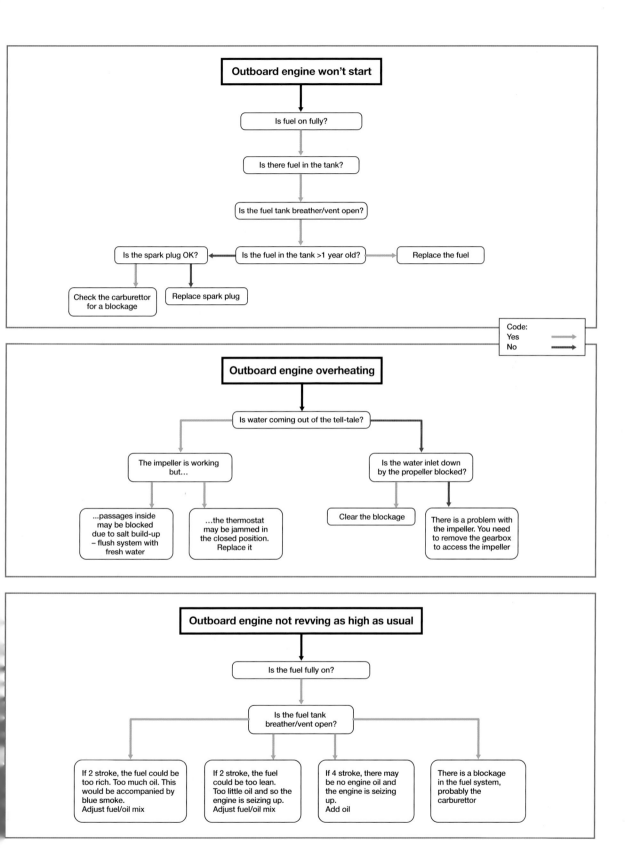

Outboard engine won't start

Is fuel on fully?

Is there fuel in the tank?

Is the fuel tank breather/vent open?

Is the spark plug OK? ← Is the fuel in the tank >1 year old? → Replace the fuel

Check the carburettor for a blockage

Replace spark plug

Code:
Yes →
No ➤

Outboard engine overheating

Is water coming out of the tell-tale?

The impeller is working but…

Is the water inlet down by the propeller blocked?

…passages inside may be blocked due to salt build-up – flush system with fresh water

…the thermostat may be jammed in the closed position. Replace it

Clear the blockage

There is a problem with the impeller. You need to remove the gearbox to access the impeller

Outboard engine not revving as high as usual

Is the fuel fully on?

Is the fuel tank breather/vent open?

If 2 stroke, the fuel could be too rich. Too much oil. This would be accompanied by blue smoke.
Adjust fuel/oil mix

If 2 stroke, the fuel could be too lean. Too little oil and so the engine is seizing up.
Adjust fuel/oil mix

If 4 stroke, there may be no engine oil and the engine is seizing up.
Add oil

There is a blockage in the fuel system, probably the carburettor

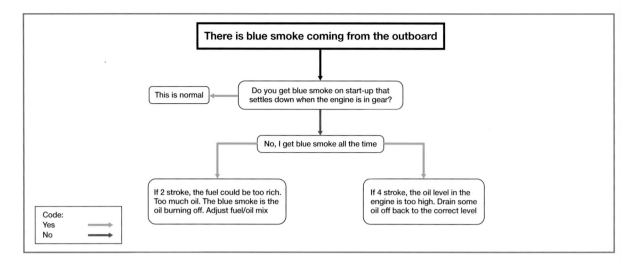

There is blue smoke coming from the outboard

Do you get blue smoke on start-up that settles down when the engine is in gear?

This is normal

No, I get blue smoke all the time

If 2 stroke, the fuel could be too rich. Too much oil. The blue smoke is the oil burning off. Adjust fuel/oil mix

If 4 stroke, the oil level in the engine is too high. Drain some oil off back to the correct level

Code:
Yes
No

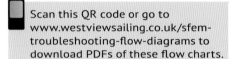

Scan this QR code or go to www.westviewsailing.co.uk/sfem-troubleshooting-flow-diagrams to download PDFs of these flow charts.

Tips and secrets to reliability

Use an air pump to unblock a raw-water inlet

If you think your raw-water inlet is blocked, use an air pump, the one you would pump a dinghy up with, and use air pressure down the raw-water inlet to unblock it. Most of the time this can be done via the raw-water strainer.

Refitting the impeller cover? Start with one screw

When you refit an impeller cover, put one screw through the hole in the plate and gasket and screw this one on first. You will find it less fiddly and you can then line up the gasket and other screws much more easily.

Refitting a used impeller

If you refit a used impeller, coat it in washing-up liquid. This will lubricate the impeller until the water flows and you can tell it is working as you will see bubbles from the exhaust in the water, especially useful if you cannot see the water outlet. A new impeller kit normally comes with a glycerine gel to lubricate the impeller when fitting. This does not produce bubbles from the exhaust so if it is hard to see your water outlet, put a bit of washing-up liquid on as well.

▲ Repaint the engine annually.

Checking that raw water is passing through the heat exchanger

On engines that have heat exchangers, the raw-water outlet to the exhaust should always be cold to touch. If it's warm then you are not getting enough raw water through the system. This may result in the engine temperature increasing at higher revs.

Paint your engine

Clean off any flaking paint from the engine and repaint annually to prevent corrosion.

How to tell if the raw-water impeller shaft seal needs replacing?

You should change the raw-water pump impeller shaft seal every other year as these regularly fail and cause the water pump to start leaking. The raw-water pump has a hole at the back to allow the water to escape when the seal is worn so the water does not go into the bearing and damage it. If you spot a leak from the pump, put your finger where the back of the pump is and if it gets wet the shaft seal needs replacing.

Fuel

Keep fuel tank as full as practical to prevent condensation forming. Use a fuel additive to prevent bug. Check seals on fuel filler caps for damage and tightness. Inspect fuel pre-filter regularly (monthly, depending on use). Remove contaminants.

Drive belt

Check for belt dust and signs of wear. Tighten or replace if required.

Batteries

Check battery water levels. Check for distortion, gassing or sulphur smell when on charge. If you notice any of these, isolate the batteries and turn the charger off. Battery replacement required.

Cleanliness is next to, er...

Keep the engine bay and bilges clean and dry to stop damp around the engine. A clean bilge allows you to spot small leaks, easily – before they become big leaks.

The engine

Regular all-round visual checks are essential, noting any deterioration. Service as per the manufacturer's instructions.

Coat the engine with corrosion inhibitor regularly to prevent rust, this can be achieved by touching up the engine's painted surfaces and then spraying a lubricant

such as Corrosion Block, which is like a thick WD-40 and can be used on metal, electrical connections and plastic. Avoid using on rubber components where a silicone grease can be used to keep these supple.

Don't run the engine for long periods at full power as this will create excessive pressure and wear to the engine. About 80–90 per cent of full throttle is adequate.

Accelerate gently to prevent overloading the engine and causing unnecessary stress to the engine components.

Here's a thought. Water in the bilges? Let's taste it.

- *Fresh?* It's probably come from the domestic fresh water system.
- *Fresh and sweet?* It's probably coolant from the engine fresh water cooling system.
- *Salty?* It's probably a leak from outside the boat. Have a look at the raw water side of the engine cooling system – raw water pump, piping, heat exchanger, strainer, raw water sea cock inlet.

You could of course use a PH testing kit to tell you if it was fresh or salty. And bilge water could be poisonous so wet your finger and give it a quick taste with your tongue and then rinse your mouth out with fresh water. Do not swallow the bilge water!

Above all...

Use the boat as much as possible – for your own enjoyment and to keep all the components in good working order and prevent seizing.

13 Spares and tools

Most boatowners carry spares for their engines on board, so what spares do you really need? It can be confusing and you end up either having none at all or enough to rebuild the engine three times over!

You need to consider:

1. What are you capable of doing – mechanically?
2. Where are you going in your boat and for how long?

What spares to carry

Below is a list of the minimum requirement for spare engine parts. I say minimum because I would consider that all of these spare parts can be replaced by the boatowner. You should have a basic understanding of how to use all these spares and these are all straightforward to fit.

But how many other spares you might also carry depends on where you are going and how far you are intending to travel. For example, if you are sailing locally, just off the coast in a popular sailing area, there is always assistance nearby if something breaks on the engine and there are plenty of places to get spare parts. So just having the basic spares is sufficient for quick fixes and getting yourself going again.

As you move further afield, so help will take longer to get to you and spares may be harder to come by.

Of course, if you are travelling across the Atlantic, your engine won't start and you can't charge the batteries – we will assume that none of your auxiliary-power generator systems, wind generator, hydro generator or solar panels is able to charge the batteries – it can end up being life-threatening. So, you would carry a spare starter motor, alternator and enough spares so you can almost rebuild your engine if you needed to and

you have the ability. If you are thousands of miles from port, you need to be able to fix things yourself.

So, the number of spare parts you carry is related to how you use the boat and your sailing area. Remember, any spares that are kept on board will be prone to corrosion and will degrade with age, so try to rotate your spares. For example, at an engine service, replace the old impeller with the spare and then buy a new one as the spare.

◆ Spares - the minimum requirement

- oil (engine, gearbox, PAS and power trim)
- oil filter × 1
- fuel pre-filter elements × 2
- fuel fine filter/elements
- drive belt(s) – 1 for each type of belt fitted as some engines can have up to 4 different belts
- impeller × 2
- fuses (check types required)
- pre-mixed antifreeze (5 litres of 50/50mix)

▲ *Impeller kit with gasket, O-ring and lubricant.*

▲ Oils

▲ Oil filter

▲ Fuel pre-filter elements

▲ Engine fuel filter

▲ Outboard petrol engine fuel filter element

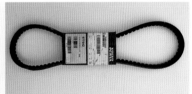

▲ Drive belt

▲ Electrical connectors, always useful. ▲ Always carry a selection of spare fuses. ▲ Don't forget coolant for topping up.

Tools

The key with tools is having the right tool for the job. Working with the wrong tool will be frustrating. Working with the right tool will make the job much easier.

And we don't need zillions of tools, just a few will do. Many boats have the most extensive tool kits on board, much of which is never used and simply rusts away. Certainly, I have a far better selection of tools on my boat than I have at home.

So, what tools do we really need?

The short answer is to carry only those tools you require to do the jobs that you will need to, for general maintenance as well as in a breakdown situation. Get to know your engine and learn how to change the spare parts yourself while safely tied up alongside with all the time in the world to work out how best to do it.

I could list tools for each job. Take the impeller, for example. I would advise a screwdriver for removing the impeller cover, an impeller puller for removing the impeller, a bucket to catch any leaking water etc. In reality, however, there is never room for the bucket; the cover of the impeller may be only 2 inches from a bulkhead, so a screwdriver will not fit on to the screw heads and an impeller puller won't fit either. For this you will need different tools entirely and may even need to remove the whole pump to be able to replace the impeller.

It makes much more sense to start with a variety of tools and then remove the ones you don't need to use once you have experienced changing components. So, learning how to change the spares you are carrying is very important. It teaches you to change the parts efficiently, which will pay dividends when in a pressured breakdown situation.

But to give you a head start, I always have the following tools:

- A socket set ranging from 7mm (really handy for most jubilee clips) to 24mm for crankshaft pulleys to be able to turn the engine by hand. These will normally have 3 different sizes of ratchet, extensions and even screwdriver bits.
- A set of flat-head and cross-head screwdrivers, from short, dumpy ones for when space is tight to large flat-bladed ones, which are useful for tightening some drive belts.
- Pliers, long nose pliers and a plumber's wrench. I also use long nose mole grips.

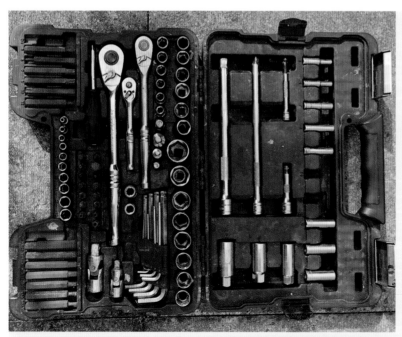

▲ Metric socket set.

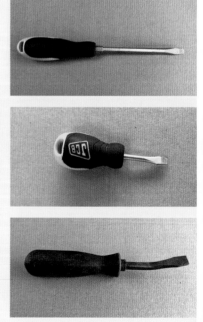

▲ Screwdrivers and lever bar.

- A set of spanners from 8mm to 24mm. Make sure they are ring spanners that are open ended one end and a ring the other. I particularly like ratcheting spanners where the ring end is ratcheted so you don't have to keep taking it off and on a bolt head constantly – very handy if there is little room to move.
- A rubber hammer, good for loosening components without damaging and it doesn't rust!
- A small, sharp scraper – useful for removing the old gasket from the impeller cover and impeller housing.
- A multimeter for checking electrics, needs to be 12V DC.
- A filter strap for removing oil and fuel filters, preferably made from metal as metal has a better grip. You can also get large open-mouthed pliers, which are specially made to undo filters.
- An impeller puller, which will fit your engine impeller, of course.
- A torch.
- Lots of paper towel.
- Gloves – never use latex as they will disintegrate when in contact with fuel and oil. Nitrile gloves work best or vinyl will do.
- I also use puppy training mats to lay on the floor as they are absorbent and have a waterproof back, which keeps spills contained.

▲ Long nose pliers and ordinary pliers.

▲ Ring spanners, one with a ratchet and angle adjustment.

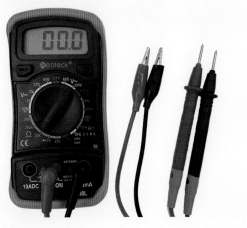

▲ Multimeter.

▲ Rubber hammer.

▲ Small scraper.

▲ Filter wrenches: strap rubber wrench; metal strap wrench and heavy-duty wrench.

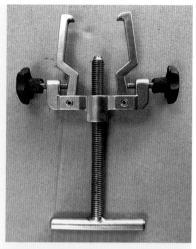

▲ An impeller puller.

▲ Torches – the small torch is for when space is limited.

▲ Paper towel.

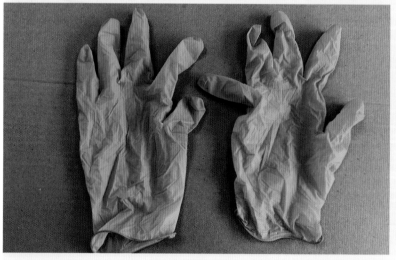

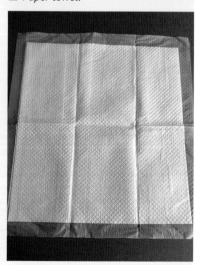

▲ Nitrile powderless gloves – don't use latex gloves as oil degrades them quickly.

▲ Fluid absorbing mat.

▲ Electrical crimping tool, top; and electrical wire stripping and crimping tool in one.

▲ Ear protectors.

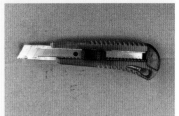

▲ Adjustable spanner capable of opening to 24mm, top; and retractable knife for cutting pipes.

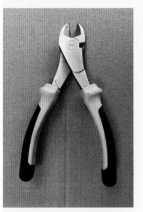

▲ Side cutters for cutting wire cable ties, pipe.

▲ Long nose mole grips.

▲ Electrical screwdriver with plastic sleeve to prevent short circuits.

▲ Electrical tape, top; and green scourer for cleaning surfaces such as the impeller plate/cover.

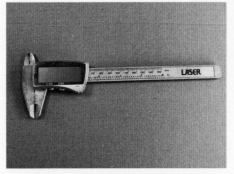

▲ A vernier calliper gauge. If you want to measure the diameter of anything – a shaft bolt, say – there is nothing else that does the job.

▲ If you intend to service your engine you will need one of these. It comes with different diameter pipes to fit the various diameters of oil dipstick holes, which you will poke the pipe down to drain the oil from the sump.

Jonathan says

Not having the right tools and spares at the right time can end up costing you time and money and can be upsetting to others around you, as you will see.

I have to admit this time the story is about me. It was I who made the mistakes and who learned the lesson. It was a number of years ago, before I joined the marine industry, when I was an RAC breakdown mechanic. My girlfriend, now my wife, and I had recently bought our second ever boat, a Fletcher 21 GTS speedboat, which was in lovely condition.

We had already enjoyed a few trips out in it and all was going well. One evening, however, in the height of summer, we decided to have a run over to Cowes on the Isle of Wight for dinner. It was dusk as we returned, heading back to our mooring in Southampton.

We were belting along and the Red Jet (the fast ferry from the IoW to Southampton) was nearby. It gives off a bit of a wash and we needed to get to the other side of it, so I decided to turn behind and go over its wash. We took off over the wash and as we landed fairly heavily, so the engine gauges all started flickering. The dials went crazy and then the engine cut out! We found ourselves in the middle of the shipping channel at dusk with no power and no lights.

'Don't worry,' I said. 'It looks electrical, let me take a look.'

I opened the engine bay, nothing obvious, all the electrics were attached, but it was becoming harder to see as it was getting dark. I then thought it could be an ignition problem as the gauges had all gone crazy before the engine cut out and remembering that the ignition fuse is behind the gauges, I decided to unscrew the gauge cluster.

At this point my (future) wife reminded me that we were in fact still in a shipping lane, that it was getting dark and we didn't have any navigation lights.

'Don't worry. All I need to do is take the gauges out and I'll just change the fuse,' I said.

'Do we have any fuses on board?' she asked.

'Ah, good point,' was my reply.

'How are you going to remove the gauge cluster, we don't have any tools on board either,' she pointed out.

'I have a penknife!' I said.

She glared at me.

At this point we looked up to see a rather large container ship leaving Southampton docks and heading, you guessed it, straight towards us. It was a couple of miles away so we radioed Southampton Harbourmaster and informed them of our predicament, which they then relayed to the ship so they knew we were in their way.

We then called Solent Coastguard on the radio and they very impressively and quickly contacted Calshot Rescue and informed us that they were on their way. Luckily for us, we drifted to the edge of the shipping channel but it was getting pretty dark now. As the ship approached, so did our rescuers. What a relief! They arrived in a small rescue RIB with four of them aboard, and they duly took us under tow all the way to Southampton, where they dropped us off at Ocean Village Marina. Forever grateful, we thanked them, praised them for their efficiency, emptied our pockets as a donation and locked up the boat.

We did, however, keep the boat out of the water at Southampton Dry Stack, not at Ocean Village. At this time of night the Dry Stack would be locked up and everyone would have gone home, and our car in the car park would now be behind locked gates. So, I called Bill, the man who runs the Dry Stack, and being the great guy that he is, he picked us up and took us back to get our car. We felt very guilty, of course, and again would be forever grateful.

The next day I went back to the boat in my RAC van. Yes, I know, I am almost embarrassed to admit it, I should have known better. Now with some tools, a torch and no pressure, I very quickly, in fact in five minutes, found the positive battery cable to the alternator had worn through on the alternator body and was shorting out. Simply moving it away allowed the engine to power up and work again. Repairing the wire and rerouting it permanently fixed the issue.

I managed to do this in about 15 minutes, where the previous night because I had no torch and no tools, we had drifted in a shipping lane for an hour, we had been a hazard to shipping, we had to get volunteers out of their homes to come and rescue us and finally we had to get poor Bill back from a hard day at work to pick us up.

I learned an important lesson that day and I even joined Sea Start – the RAC of the water – the next day. This moment, incidentally, also changed my career as two years later I left the RAC, having worked there for seven years, and joined Sea Start as an engineer. I stayed there for a further ten years and then started my own marine engineering company, Parker Marine Services, to teach boatowners how to look after their engines and prevent breaking down.

Ironic, don't you think?

Glossary

Cambelt Connects the crankshaft to the camshaft.

Camshaft Operates the valves for the air inlet and the exhaust outlet.

Circulation pump Run off the drive belt, this pumps coolant round the closed system, just like a central heating pump.

Coolant Fresh-water and antifreeze mix – usually 50/50.

Crankshaft Drives the pistons and the camshaft, and via the drive belt, drives the alternator and the coolant circulation pump.

Diode A semi-conductor – a one-way switch for current, allowing it to pass in one direction but not in the other.

Diode splitter Splits the charge in two to allow two batteries to be charged at once from one source.

Drive belt A belt that connects the crankshaft to other components that require turning to operate, eg the alternator, water pumps, power-steering pump and supercharger.

Heat exchanger A device that exchanges heat from one medium to another. Here, the coolant, warmed by the engine, is then cooled by the raw water as it passes through the heat exchanger.

Heat exchanger bundle Series of pipes through which the raw water flows within the heat exchanger.

Impeller The rotating component within the pump that, because of its design and vanes, pushes the water around the system.

Lift pump 'Lifts' or sucks the fuel from the fuel tank and pumps it to the high-pressure diesel fuel pump or petrol carburettor, depending on engine type.

Raw water Sea water, river water or lake water.

Raw-water pump Run off the engine, this pumps the sea water, lake water, river water around the system, through the heat exchanger to cool the coolant in the closed system.

Sea cock A valve set into the hull of a boat, which can be opened and closed. Types of valve: screw-in gate valve or lever and ball valve.

Starter relay Relays the charge from the ignition to the starter solenoid.

Starter solenoid Activates the starter motor.

Index